MARKS & SPENCER
1884-1984

MARKS & SPENCER
1884 ~ 1984

QTY	DESCRIPTION	PRICE
1	A Centenary History of Marks & Spencer	1d

THE ORIGINATORS OF
PENNY BAZAARS

ASA BRIGGS

for
ANGELA,
a special customer among 14 million customers

ACKNOWLEDGEMENTS

The writing of this book would have been impossible had it not been for the help at every stage of Paul Bookbinder. He has not only guided me through the M & S archives, which he personally has done much to assemble, but has arranged meetings for me with a large number of people inside the company – too many, indeed, to mention by name. His enthusiasm has been as great a source of inspiration to me as his knowledge; so, too, has his relentless curiosity.

I am deeply grateful to the President, Chairman and members of the Board, to the management, and to many M & S employees, past and present, in the provinces as well as in London, who have often gone to great trouble to make themselves and the information at their disposal freely available. Both their oral and their written reminiscences have illuminated my research, and they have given me a warm sense of belonging. John Salisse, in particular, has made me feel that sense from beginning to end, and he has introduced me also to many M & S suppliers who share the company's philosophy of business. I would also like to thank Adrian Shire.

Within Octopus Books I was given the same kind of welcome from Margaret McLean, and Kit Coppard and his colleagues have been immensely helpful. I would especially like to thank Ann Lunan, who has been responsible for typing a number of versions of the text, often in far from easy circumstances. She has shown great forbearance as well as diligence.

Finally, I would like to thank the many librarians and museum curators who are necessary and committed colleagues in producing a book of this kind. They have answered difficult queries and supplied what has often been out-of-the-way evidence.

This is a very special centenary, and I hope that the publication of my book will lead to the unearthing of information which has been lost. There is no finality about the writing of history.

ASA BRIGGS

Oxford, 1984

First published in 1984 by
Octopus Books Limited
59 Grosvenor Street, London, W1
© Hennerwood Publications Limited

ISBN 0 906320 05 4

Designed by Trickett & Webb Limited
Printed and bound by
Jarrold & Sons Limited, Norwich

MARKS AND SPENCER
1884-1984

CONTENTS

FROM LORD SIEFF OF BRIMPTON

We at Marks and Spencer are marking our Centenary with projects of value to the Community given by the Company but chosen by the staff of each store. The staff unasked have raised considerable funds further to develop these projects.

This involvement in the Community stems from a concern for the individual that began with Michael Marks, the founder of the Business. Out of his concern for the individual came an approach to people which has made an important contribution to better human relations in industry.

The M & S story cannot be told away from its social context. Who better then to tell it than Asa Briggs, whose chief study has been the social history of Britain in the last hundred years?

His book is a fascinating account of men of vision and determination like my grandfather, Michael Marks, my uncle, Simon Marks, and my father, Israel Sieff. It is a story too of level-headed businessmen like Tom Spencer and, of course, of the staff, customers and suppliers, without whom there would be no Marks and Spencer.

Lord Briggs explains how the philosophy developed by my predecessors has been the foundation on which our Company has progressed. His book is packed with intriguing detail and enriched by some very good photographs, many of which have never been published before.

I believe this book will appeal to all interested in the times in which we live. It will be treasured by many who, like me, have worked for Marks and Spencer.

Sieff of Brimpton

Lord Sieff of Brimpton OBE MA
22nd June 1984

SIMON MARKS AND A PAGE FROM HIS ACCOUNT OF THE COMPANY'S EARLY YEARS

A NATION OF CUSTOMERS

There are many different ways of telling a story. Sometimes a chronicler or narrator who has not been directly involved tells it from outside. Sometimes a story-teller draws on his own memories and recalls his experiences in the past.

The fascinating story of the largest retail organisation in Britain, M & S (as it is usually known inside and outside the business), has already received both kinds of treatment from story-tellers. In 1969 Goronwy Rees, an outsider, published his *St Michael, A History of Marks and Spencer*, tracing the origin and development of the business through two generations. He began with Michael Marks's opening of a penny stall on a trestle table in Leeds market in 1884 – he is said to have paid 18 pence for the privilege – and he ended with the death of Simon (Lord) Marks in 1964, by which time M & S turnover was £201 million.

Simon Marks had been Chairman of the company, which was founded in 1903, for nearly 50 years, and he, too, had tried his hand at story-telling from within. A brief, undated and unpublished manuscript of his takes the reader forward from the death of his pioneering father, Michael, the founder of the business, in 1907 through to the 1920s, when Simon was transforming the business with the help of his great friend Israel (later Lord) Sieff. 'My wife holds the view', he began, 'that a stranger should write the story and that it is a conceit which drives me to undertake the task myself'. Fortunately, however, Simon was not diverted from his story-telling. 'Who better than myself?', he asked. 'For whilst I am penning these lines, I am reliving the story'. He added cautiously, however, that he felt that it would interest few people 'outside my own immediate circle'. It would be of main value to members of his own family, 'if not of this generation, of a great grandchild who will have heard of me only as a legend'.

It was characteristic of Simon Marks to relate his work to his family, for M & S was – and is – a business with a strong family sense. The story of the business, indeed, is, in many of its crucial episodes, the story of the family (and of many other families, too, at different levels of the business). Yet Simon greatly underestimated the appeal of the story to people outside his own family. After all, the story of M & S is intimately bound up with the history not only of the family but of the nation, and not only of the nation but of other nations also.

As one of the first numbers of *St Michael News*, a lively house journal for the staff of M & S, put it in 1954, 'Marks and Spencer is news to the general public'. And that was on the eve of the so-called 'age of affluence', of which it was said by a writer in *Punch* (in June 1963) that St Michael was the patron saint. In the same year Harry Hopkins in his highly readable social history of the 1940s and 1950s, *The New Look*, spoke of 'a Marksian revolution ... in the logic of the times'. Three years later another writer was to discover 'inimitable magic' in the story; and Anthony Sampson, knowledgeable author of *The Anatomy of Britain*, was not alone in applying the adjective 'legendary' to M & S in 1971. By then the famous Marble Arch store, which features in the *Guinness Book of Records* for the highest sales taken per square metre, had acquired a world-wide reputation in its own right.

The trade-mark St Michael, which figures not only on M & S labels but in almost everything that has recently been written about the firm, had first been used in 1928, but at that time it was applied only to a strictly limited range of M & S textile products – 'shirts, pyjamas and knitted articles of clothing'. Mackintoshes followed in 1931, toys and games in 1932, and india-rubber hot-water bottles in 1936. The first food product registered under the name was margarine in 1940. It was not until 1949, when M & S was more than half a century old, that Simon Marks first referred to it in his Chairman's speech. By then, the trade-mark had also been registered abroad in 16 countries, Switzerland leading the way in 1947.

Wherever the name was adopted and whatever the product named, the St Michael label became both a gilt-edged guarantee to customers of standards of quality and value and a part of the legend of which Simon Marks wrote in his unpublished manuscript about the history of M & S. After all, it was the first name of the founder of the business.

In the story of any successful business with a long history, there are often elements of philosophy and there are always elements of legend. Anecdotes multiply even when crucial records do not exist. Nonetheless, there are perhaps more elements of philosophy and of legend in the story of M & S than in the story of most successful businesses. The legend begins with the mystery surrounding the very early history of Michael and the romance of his business partnership with Tom Spencer, who joined him in 1894, and folklore and fact still meet at the surviving M & S stall in Grainger Market, Newcastle-on-Tyne, the smallest store in the business and the one which in appearance most resembles the early bazaars.

The philosophy begins with Simon Marks and with *his* partnership – intellectual and social as well as commercial – with Israel Sieff, an exact contemporary at Manchester Grammar School. It was a philosophy formulated in its essentials between the time that Israel joined the M & S board in 1915 and the time that he became Vice-Chairman and Assistant Managing Director in 1926. Both Simon and Israel, whose minds complemented each other, propounded it with

Right: Documents relating to the registration in 1928 of the trade names 'St Michael' and 'St Joan'. The registration of 'St Joan' was never completed.

conviction and force, and it was in a natural succession that Israel became Chairman of M & S in 1964 after Simon's death.

The philosophy, known to all in the business and many outside it, was well summed up by Israel in 1966. It rested on six principles, expressed in terms of the objectives enumerated in the margin (*below right*).

On the eve of his retirement as Chief Executive of M & S in 1983, after 10 years of remarkable expansion, Lord Sieff, Israel's son Marcus, insisted that although the retail business was 'ever-changing', the principles and objectives had never changed since they were first formulated. What had changed, of course, was the social context in which they were applied and the sense of the best means of implementing them. Who in the early 1960s, however, inside the business – let alone outside – could have anticipated at the time of Simon's death that within 20 years, less than the span of a generation, M & S turnover net of VAT would be over £2000 million? The legendary future in M & S has always been even more exciting than the legendary past.

As I have dug deep into the fragmentary but always richly rewarding M & S archives, I have talked to people inside the business and visited a wide range of stores and a rather narrower range of suppliers, and I have necessarily been concerned as a professional historian with facts rather than with legends. Yet I confess that my desire to tell the story has been prompted by the knowledge that the people who have made M & S what it is have always been concerned not only with facts, essential though these are to a businessman (as the Economic Information Department of M & S demonstrates), but with vision.

In this connection one of the aspects of the story which I have found most absorbing is the relationship between the generality of the M & S philosophy, which has a relevance far outside the company, and the daily detail of the scattered retail business. On stalls or in bazaars or in stores or in super-stores – and these have been the successive and very different selling points of the evolving M & S business – everything that is sold has a history of its own. It ranges from that of the hairpins and dolly dyes and black lead on the first stalls to the bracelets and baking tins and wooden dolls of the bazaars (a dying word), to the rayon dresses and poplin shirts and pork pies and Jaffa oranges of the stores, and to the cropped-length women's trousers and reversible coats and crispy lettuces and foam baths of the 262 modern super-stores, where 14 million people shop each week. There is a wealth of detail here, but it is part of a pattern. Of course, the history of M & S products is the history of the people who make them, the people who select them for sale, the people who transport them, the people who sell them, and, last but never least, the people who buy them.

The word 'service' has been as significant in the history of M & S as the word 'vision', for, as a leader in *St Michael News* put it in 1967, 'Without service the Company's prestige would falter'. In the first and last resort, both the vision and the service relate not to the company, but to the customer. Standard-setting and the monitoring of quality control are in the interest of the customer. So, too, is the staff policy. The 900 trained staff responsible for the welfare, training and progress of the rest of the staff, working in the stores, insist through a continuous 'Welcome to M & S' campaign that 'within M & S the central figure is the customer'.

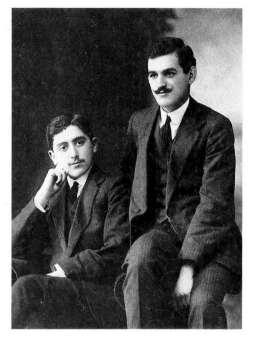

Simon Marks (left) and Israel Sieff in their twenties. They had first met in Manchester in 1901, and each would later marry the other's sister.

The six principles of the business philosophy propounded by Simon Marks and Israel Sieff:

1 To offer customers, under the company's own brand name St Michael, a selective range of high-quality, well-designed and attractive merchandise at reasonable prices.

2 To encourage suppliers to use the most modern and efficient techniques of production provided by the latest discoveries in science and technology.

3 With the cooperation of these suppliers, to enforce the highest standards of quality control.

4 To plan the expansion of the stores for the better display of a widening range of goods and for the convenience of our customers.

5 To simplify operating procedures so that the business is carried on in an efficient manner.

6 To foster good human relations with customers, suppliers and staff.

Above: The pedlar's certificate issued to Afrem Seff (Ephraim Sieff, Israel's father) in 1887, the year after he landed at Hull after fleeing from Russia. The photograph shows a street pedlar of about 1900.

There are, of course, customers of all shapes and sizes, and of all varieties of occupation and income, and they have changed greatly in their requirements, their tastes and their habits since 1884. For this reason my own emphasis in telling this story is not on M & S as a case study in business history but on the customers who buy what M & S sell, and that is why I have chosen *A Nation of Customers* as my chapter title. Behind the title, however, there is an older story than that of M & S. Napoleon once called England 'a nation of shopkeepers'. And although that was nearly 200 years ago – before shopkeepers, big or small, had come into their own – there was a sense in which he was right. While there were elaborate hierarchies of 'dealers', from packmen and pedlars to sophisticated and expensive London shopkeepers, and while there were almost as many prices (often the result of higgling) as there were products, already some men of vision then saw that the future would be different. 'We think it is of far more consequence', wrote one of them in 1796, before Napoleon had won any of his great victories, 'to supply the People than the Nobility only; and though you speak contemptuously of Hawkers, Pedlars and those who supply *Petty Shops*, yet we think they will do more towards supporting a great manufacturing business than all the Lords in the nation'.

Michael Marks, who started as a pedlar before he set up his stall and described himself on his marriage certificate as a hawker, lived long enough to set up 60 branches of M & S. He was one of the key figures in the first real transformation in retailing in the late nineteenth century and the prelude to the still greater transformation in the last decades of the twentieth century. It was only under the direction of his son Simon and of Israel Sieff, however, that there was recognition of the full social implications of operating a nation-wide retail business designed to attract the widest possible section of the population.

In order that the use of the term 'nation of customers' could become possible, three developments were necessary. First, a high proportion of the total population had to have enough disposable money in their pockets to spend on items other than the bare necessities of life. Second, there had to be enough goods available to meet people's growing range of wants. This meant an increase in production – in the fields as well as in the factories, abroad as well as in Britain – and an improvement in transport, national and international. Third, there had to be shopkeepers who were interested in satisfying not only the explicit demands of a few customers but the as yet unspoken wants of millions of customers.

A few months before Michael Marks opened his stall in Leeds market, Dr (later Sir) Robert Giffen, the President of the Statistical (later the Royal Statistical) Society, addressed his colleagues on 'the progress of the working classes in the last half century', what he called elsewhere 'a revolution of the most remarkable description'.

During the previous 50 years, he claimed, while prices had remained much the same as they had been, there had been an enormous rise in money wages, ranging from 20% in some cases to as much as 50 to 100% in others, and in one or two instances to more than 100%. And since bread, in particular – and it was very much the staple commodity then – had become cheaper, more money was left to spend on far more varied items of food and on other items. Moreover, 'there were many new things in existence at a low price which would not then have been bought at all'. Only meat was more expensive, but then meat had scarcely figured in working men's diets a half century before, when they 'had little more concern with its price than with the price of diamonds'.

Nonetheless, Giffen was not complacent. First, he noted that there was a large section of the population, a 'residuum', whose position was still unimproved. Second, he was aware of the fact, although not of its full implications, that while there was 'great diffusion of wealth', wealth was still very unevenly divided. Third, he appreciated that *how* people spent their incomes, not just how *much* they had to spend, affected their material benefits: there was 'an art of spending, a subject of separate enquiry'. Fourth, there was still much to be achieved: 'No one can contemplate the conditions of the masses of the people without desiring something like a revolution for the latter'. The revolution that had already taken place was to be followed by another.

Over a century that revolution, to use Giffen's language, has come – and it is described in my story. Yet although both standards of life and ways of life in 1884 and in 1984 contrast dramatically – with some problems, such as unemployment, having grown in importance – it is perhaps more accurate to call what has happened a continuing evolution, which has gone through many difficult phases, rather than a revolution. Inside M & S itself the stress has always been on 'organic growth' – on innovation and adaptation.

The years between 1954 and 1964 stand out in the story as the years of breakthrough not only from an 'age of austerity' into an 'age of affluence' but from one set of value systems into another. It was in 1954, the last year of the war-time rationing regulations, that the Chancellor of the Exchequer, R.A. (later Lord) Butler, told the electorate that the country should aim at doubling its standard of living within the next 25 years. Although there were many people who believed such an aim to be unrealistic, the annual rate of growth of the national product was in fact to average 2.6% for the next 20 years, a higher rate than in the late-Victorian years which Giffen lived through.

Between 1955 and 1960, the golden years of advertising – and it is significant that broadly speaking M & S did not advertise to increase sales – there was a striking growth in the number of motor-cars on the roads, up from 3½ to 5½ million. The percentage of the population with driving licences rose from 18 to 32. For ownership of washing machines, the percentage rose from 25 to 44 and of refrigerators from 6 to 16; the number of television sets rose from 4½ to 10½ million. And the increases continued throughout the 1960s.

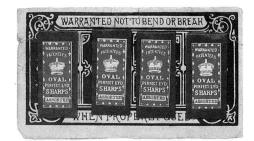

All these were so-called 'durable consumer goods', many of them of American origin, which M & S did not stock. Yet the remarkable leap of M & S ahead of its competitors can be traced back to those years. Turnover rose from £95 million in 1954 to £148 million in 1960, while the abolition of building controls in 1954 enabled a long-delayed building programme to be launched. Stores began to look different both outside and, more importantly, inside. And customers were changing even more than the stores. They were earning more, spending more, and, most important of all, expecting more.

Between 1956 and 1961 M & S food sales rose from £17 million to £28 million (17% of M & S total sales). As to textiles, there were many signs of a change in customers' attitudes during the 1950s, when there was a revulsion against wartime restrictions.

Of course, there were limits to the affluence, and darker sides to the success story itself. There were economic problems much discussed at the time, problems which were to grow. Although by 1970 industrial production was 30% greater than it had been in 1960 and 80% greater than it had been in 1950, Britain's rate of growth was only 60% that of other industrial countries.

There was a note of introspection, therefore, rather than of confidence during the late 1960s and early 1970s which it was not easy to dispel, as 'league-table' comparisons were regularly made between the economic performance of Britain and that of other European countries. In 1961 the British gross national product was 26% of the total product of what were to become the nine member states of the European Economic Community: by 1973, when Britain joined 'the Nine', it was down to 19%. Moreover, retail prices rose by more than 50% between 1953 and 1967. M & S was held up as a model in such circumstances not only because, whatever the national trends, its performance was so striking, but because it was always anxious both to buy British and to advertise Britain abroad. Between 1975 and 1977 St Michael exports trebled, rising from £13.5 million to £40 million.

The 1970s were a particularly difficult decade for the nation as unemployment and inflation, never before linked together, rose to unprecedented post-war heights. It is significant that in these circumstances M & S was confident about the future. 'If British leadership is determined', said Lord (Marcus) Sieff in November 1982, a few months before he announced that he would hand over the tasks of Chief Executive to Lord Rayner, 'we can produce profitably at home goods of high quality and good value which today are often imported.... Our suppliers are among the best in the world'.

Contrasts in rural and urban retailing in the late 19th century: a market square (below) in a small country town and (right) Oxford Street, London in 1880.

It became clear in the early 1980s that the way to the twenty-first century would be through an economic and social transformation as dramatic in its way as the Industrial Revolution of the late eighteenth century and more far-reaching than the important long-term social developments of the last century which are part of my story.

Among those social developments was a sharp reduction in family size. Around 1870 the average number of children per family was 6, but in the last decade of the nineteenth century the number had fallen to 4.3, and in the years 1950-4, at the beginning of the consumer boom, it was down to 2.31. In 1974, a year of political crisis, the fertility rate fell to 2.04, which was below the level necessary for replacement.

Behind the fall in the birth rate was the sense that the size of the family could be controlled, and this, coupled with the longer average expectation of life, had many effects on the family. Women were increasingly freed from what, for most of them, had been a relentless cycle of family obligation, and a growing proportion of them went to work in a widening range of jobs; children were more subject to the influence of compulsory schooling (school was a relatively new phenomenon when M & S began); husbands took on new roles, many of which would have surprised their Victorian great-grandfathers (they even learned how to shop). Meanwhile, domestic service declined, labour-saving devices in the home increased, home-centred activity and entertainment were transformed with the development of sound broadcasting, record players, the motor-car, television, and video, and transport was completely reorganised. The proportion of people aged over 65 in the total population was 17% in 1981 as compared with 15% in 1961 and 5% in 1901. All in all, for every 20 people of working age in 1981 there were 13 who were either over retirement age or under the age of 16.

Painting of Marks and Spencer's stall in Ashton-under-Lyne's covered market in 1894 – the first year of the partnership.

Within this changing setting homes have come to look and to feel different, particularly during the span of the last generation. So, too, have roads, and the appearance of villages, towns and cities. The changes can be appreciated as clearly from photographs as from statistics – and that is one reason why this book includes many pictures.

Gordon Selfridge, one of the early-twentieth century pioneers of modern retailing, who had nothing to do with M & S and whose business philosophy was very different from that of Simon Marks, wrote in a thick volume called *The Romance of Commerce* (1918), in which he assessed his own experience, that retailing was 'the most interesting of all forms of business, and by its constant and necessary publicity it occupies perhaps the most conspicuous place in the public mind'. Whether he was right or not in this judgement, he was unmistakably right when he added of retailing – and it explains the emphasis of this centenary study of M & S – that it is intimately associated with every aspect of modern life.

MICHAEL MARKS (LEFT) AND TOM SPENCER, FOUNDERS OF THE COMPANY

IN THE BEGINNING

In the beginning there is usually legend. There is no birth certificate for Michael Marks, although it is said that his mother died in giving him birth at Slonim in the Russian Polish province of Grodno in June 1859. That is the date given in his naturalisation papers in 1897, although it is not certain in the absence of full immigration records just when he crossed from Russian Poland to England. His name does not figure in the 1881 census return, nor in any other leading documents of the 1880s. Tom Spencer, who was born in Skipton, Yorkshire, can be timed and placed more precisely. He was born on 7 November 1851, the year of the Great Exhibition, and he had moved to Leeds before he was 21. After the death of his first wife, he married again in 1892, two years before he entered his partnership with Marks.

Marks and Spencer came together, Jew and Gentile, in the pursuit of enterprise, but they would never have met had it not been for persecution. Tsar Alexander II's anti-semitic pogroms (the Russian word *pogrom* means destruction) had driven 2 million Jews from the vast territories that Russia controlled. Some 130,000 displaced Jews came from there to Britain during the late nineteenth century, among them Michael and, a few years later in 1890, his brother Ephraim, who lived until 1940. (Ephraim's daughter is still alive, aged 98.)

By the time Marks and Spencer came together in 1894, Michael had already carved out a new life in the retail trade. It must have had a difficult and precarious beginning, for he spoke no English, had no capital, and knew no trade. Nor was he physically strong. It seems most likely that he first made his way not to the industrial city of Leeds, a city of 'muck and brass', where there was a growing Jewish population of over 6,000 people – and where he was to meet Spencer – but farther north. What evidence exists suggests that he landed not in London or Hull but in Hartlepool (County Durham), where he may have slept on the floor in the local synagogue for a few nights before he turned to the itinerant trade of peddling; and when he began to peddle it may have been, not in the Yorkshire dales of the West Riding, as previous historians have suggested, but to the north-east in the area round Stockton-on-Tees.

Peddling or hawking, one of the oldest forms of retailing, was an arduous and demanding trade which was to survive in England into the twentieth century, as were some of the centuries-old urban markets where buyers and sellers gathered in the open air. There is no precise documentary evidence of the date when Michael began to sell his goods on the trestle table in Leeds' Kirkgate open market, but it could not have been earlier than the last months of 1884. His stall was probably open from 9 o'clock in the morning until 7 at night on Tuesdays and until 11 on Saturdays, the two days a week to which business was restricted; and this would have left him scope on other days either for peddling or for trading in nearby markets in the West Riding, such as Castleford and Wakefield.

The first secure date in Michael Marks's new English life is not for the setting up of his stall but for his marriage on 19 November 1886 to Hannah Cohen, then 21

years old. He described himself on his marriage licence as a 'licensed hawker', and he is said to have met his wife in Stockton-on-Tees.

Their first child died in infancy. Their second child, born in 1888, was Simon; in 1915 he would marry Miriam, daughter of Ephraim Sieff, who had been born in Kovno (Russia), came to England at the age of 25 in 1886 and became a cotton and woollen rag merchant in Manchester. Miriam's brother Israel married Simon's sister Rebecca in 1910. A business dynasty was thereby founded. There were four daughters to follow Simon, and three of them would marry directors of M & S.

It seems likely that by 1886, at least, the first working philosophy of that future business dynasty had already been formulated – the product not of theory but of practice. A new covered market had been opened in Leeds in 1857, and when in 1886 Michael took up a stall inside it at a low rent it was considerably better than the trestle table in the open air. Very soon – it may even have been before the move – he was attaching a notice to all his goods on display: 'Don't Ask the Price, It's a Penny'. It was a notice with a future. The goods were simple enough – things like nails, screws, pins, needles, buttons, handkerchiefs, mending wool, reels of cotton, soaps, sponges, tumblers, cups, saucers, plates, egg cups, baking tins.

The slogan – and the policy it proclaimed in such simple words – proved irresistible. Michael pared his profits to the minimum – though they varied from article to article – in order to increase sales. Above all, shopping at the Marks stall was made easy, for everything could be seen and everything could be handled. Nor was there any haggling about the price, as there often was both in the market and on the doorstep. Stocktaking and accounting became straightforward too. There was a further advantage, carefully noted by Harry Sacher (born in 1881), who, after studying history and economics at New College, Oxford – a very different route from Michael's or Tom Spencer's – was to marry Simon's sister Miriam in 1915 and would later join the M & S business. In an unpublished history of the company, Sacher observed that 'one of the effects of a fixed price

Below: The naturalization application papers completed by Michael Marks in 1897, in which he described himself as a General Dealer.

Below, right: The market at Michael Marks's birthplace, Slonim, in Russian Poland – a photograph dating from about 1910.

M & S penny bazaar at Exeter in 1912.

list is to set the trader always on the search for greater variety and better value at that price. Under this spur, he makes discoveries which might never occur to him under a system of flexible prices.... His imagination as a buyer is activated, and he often transmits a like ingenuity to his supplier.'

In the first phase of Michael's market selling, during which 'original penny bazaars' were opened in Castleford and Wakefield as well as Leeds, two further ingredients were essential for the recipe of the penny bazaar to work. First, credit was needed. Second, there had to be human support: one man could not make a breakthrough entirely on his own. Michael Marks found both at the same time, not through impersonal agencies like a bank or an employment bureau, but through personal contact in Leeds. Within a short distance of the market, Isaac Jowitt Dewhirst of 32 Kirkgate, who was younger than Michael (he was born in 1863), had just set up a wholesale business of his own. Marks is said to have met Dewhirst while looking for work. Dewhirst not only provided him with small quantities of capital but taught him a little English as well. Through Dewhirst there was to be a more momentous link. The Dewhirst cashier was Tom Spencer, an excellent book-keeper; he was to acquire a lively and intelligent second wife, Agnes, who would help to improve Michael's English. In 1894, the year when Michael acquired a permanent stall in Leeds' covered market, he decided to invite Spencer to become his partner.

It was to be one of the most famous business partnerships in English history, better known today than that of Matthew Boulton and James Watt in Birmingham during the early years of the Industrial Revolution more than a century before. It rested on contrasting, if complementary, qualities even more than had the Boulton and Watt partnership. While Marks was endowed with imagination and spirit, Spencer was stubborn and persistent. He had a way with figures and believed in thrift. Even physically the two men were different. Marks was slight, Spencer burly.

Isaac Dewhirst (seen here in the 1930s), a wholesaler of Kirkgate, Leeds, lent Michael Marks money to acquire stock in 1884. Ten years later Marks took Dewhirst's book-keeper, Tom Spencer, into partnership: the note in Dewhirst's diary (at the top of the left-hand page) confirms Spencer's departure.

English businesses have often grown – and sometimes have broken – on the basis of such partnerships, which have involved at their best a tacit or explicit division of labour. Marks knew what he wanted in 1894, and he got it, and when Spencer contributed £300 for his half share, he unknowingly made one of the best investments of the century.

By then Michael had moved his home across the Pennines and his main penny bazaar from Leeds to Manchester (with three years in Wigan on the way), while Ephraim Marks, when he came to Britain, settled in Lancashire too – first in Accrington (as a pedlar) then in 1891 in Manchester. Wigan, Michael's first Lancashire home, was an old market centre, within easy reach of a number of Lancashire towns in which he was soon to set up bazaars – Warrington, Birkenhead and Bolton. He settled in Manchester in 1893, where he lived at first above his shop at 20 Cheetham Hill Road.

The shop was more imposing than the home, and Michael was to move house again one year later. The slogan 'Don't Ask the Price, It's a Penny' was painted in scarlet along the front, with the words 'Admission Free' added. Once inside, you could walk along a gangway six or seven feet wide, inspecting the goods for sale on open display on a horseshoe-shaped counter. You had the freedom of the store. This new bazaar was the prototype of many more to come. Customers were encouraged to go in, even if there was nothing in particular that they wanted to buy. In local markets, of course, the public had always assumed the right to browse among the stalls; but it was quite new for a shopkeeper to encourage this in his customers.

Manchester in the 1890s was still the great northern city, the original shock city of the Industrial Revolution, now firmly settled in its industrial routines, but ready for innovations in its shopping habits. It was a regional capital with more than 1½ million people living within a radius of 20 km (12 miles); a working-class city with an active business community which still largely managed the city's affairs, and a flourishing social and cultural life, reflected in the Royal Exchange, the *Manchester Guardian*, the Hallé Orchestra, and the famous grammar school, where Michael Marks's son would be educated. . It also had a thriving Jewish community of about 25,000 people. Michael was to be drawn fully into this stream of life, and into Jewish charities: he was a member, for example, of the Committee for the Soup Kitchen for the Jewish Poor.

In 1894, however, he was a newcomer, and it was probably because he sensed the opportunities not only in Manchester but in other Lancashire towns that he felt that he needed a partner. Putting together the bits and pieces of his first Lancashire business has involved laborious detective work among local market rent rolls and deeds; moreover, as a result of fire and war many crucial documents have disappeared. Already before 1890 Michael seems to have acquired stalls 8 and 9 in Warrington Market Hall; and in May 1892 he took a stall in Bolton Market. Stalls 10 and 12 at Ashton-under-Lyne followed in January 1894 at a rent of 9s 6d a week: not until 1901 did the name of the stallholder change from Michael Marks to Marks and Spencer, when the rent was raised to 20s.

In Birkenhead, as local historian W.R.S. McIntyre has discovered, it was only a few months before the M & S partnership that 'Michael Marks of Manchester' had successfully applied in March 1894 for two stalls in the central avenue of the market at a combined rent of 10s a week, and in August of the same year he

Above: Oldham Street, Manchester, where M & S had a bazaar and a store (albeit on different sites) from before the turn of the century. The present store is in Market Street.

Left: The partnership's first six female employees, photographed in about 1897. From left, Ada Probert, Laura Cowburn, Esther Brown (the first of all), Cissie Rowland, Hilda Cartwright, and Gertie Probert.

Above: Model of a penny bazaar of the early 1900s.

Below: Michael Marks's penny notebook showing the entry recording his holding in the company at the formation of the partnership.

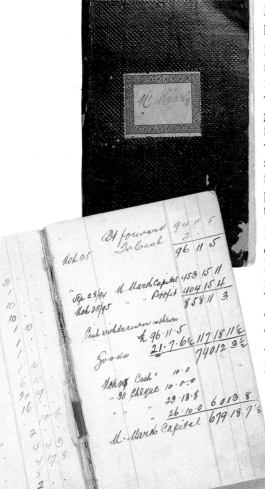

secured permission to install a gas meter (at an increased rent) to enable him to use more or brighter gas jets.

Once together, Marks and Spencer began to look further afield. At Birmingham Market Hall a store was opened in 1895 (the first record in a Birmingham directory is for 1898), as was a similar store in Grainger Market, Newcastle-upon-Tyne. In March of the same year Marks and Spencer applied to trade in Cardiff, securing three adjoining sites in the market on a three-year lease at a rent of 25s a week; they had to deposit £5 when they pulled down the partitions between them. There were new market permits in Bath, too, acquired in June 1895 (at 20s a week). Finally, in 1899, London beckoned, when the first M & S store opened at 20 London Road, Southwark, and a second (short-lived) store followed at 25 New Cut, Lambeth. All the M & S stores were now called Penny Bazaars.

Manchester was the headquarters of the whole enterprise; there a shop was opened at 63 Stretford Road in 1896, and a year later a warehouse was acquired in Robert Street (near Strangeways prison), complete with three large floors and a basement and with a hydraulic lift from the basement to the top floor. By that time many of the goods on sale were being bought directly from manufacturers, thus cutting out the profits of the middleman. They came from many different parts of Europe, including Germany, Austria and France; there is no evidence that any came from the United States, where F.W. Woolworth, not yet trading in Britain, had begun his low-fixed-price business in 1879. Woolworth first visited Europe in 1900, where he concluded that the 'little shops' he had seen were 'not much like our fine 5 and 10 cent stores'.

If direct buying from manufacturers, said to have been suggested to Michael Marks by Dewhirst, who was a wholesaler, was to become a key element in future M & S strategy, there were signs also of the other key element in the future M & S philosophy of the business: sensible and sensitive staffing.

From the moment that two market stalls had to be open on the same day, Marks needed staff, and he engaged Esther Brown, one of two female assistants already in his service, to work one of the stalls while he worked the other. Delegation was merely the first step; personal care for the assistants, in a field of business not greatly given to care, was the second. While Spencer, with the help of one foreman, was supervising with great firmness the 20 staff in the warehouse, which was under his control, Marks was putting up wooden platforms for girls to stand on in the market halls so that their feet would not get cold. He was sharing food with them and giving them Christmas presents, and as soon as he opened penny bazaar shops he provided gas rings on which the girl assistants could heat their lunches.

In 1901 a new warehouse was built to the partners' own design in Derby Street, off Cheetham Hill Road. The cost of the new building is not known, but it would have been far beyond the partners' means in 1894 when, against Spencer's initial investment of £300, Marks had held £453 15s 11d – as precise a figure as any Victorian accountant could have wished for. Within a few months, the Marks capital had deliberately been reduced through drawings to £300 so that the stake of the two partners in the business was identical.

Two small black penny notebooks survive – one labelled 'Mr. Marks', one 'Mr. Spencer' – setting out the details of the trading fortunes of the two men from

September 1894 to January 1898. In just over three years their initial capital of £753 15s 11d increased to £5,000, a net figure after substantial personal drawings by each of them of over £2,000.

There are few detailed figures of store takings before 1901, but one precious notebook survives from the Sunderland bazaar, which opened on 2 November 1895. It was kept by an M & S manageress, Mrs Thornton. The first day's takings – on a Thursday – were 3s 8d and the second day's £10 13s 2d: in the week before Christmas the weekly takings were £60 7s 3d. The following year, in a week which included Christmas Day, they were actually slightly down. On 23 May 1898 the name Mr Marks appears against the day's total of £3 2s 7d. Did he visit Sunderland on that day? The last entry is for July 1898.

Two years later, there is evidence that M & S had penny bazaars in 23 market halls and 'branch establishments' in 11 other places. The halls included Bath, Glossop, Huddersfield, Hartlepool, Middlesbrough, Rotherham, Stalybridge, Sheffield, Southport, St Helens, Scarborough, Warrington, and Wolverhampton; and among the 11 'branch establishments' were Stretford Road and Oldham Street in Manchester, Blackpool, Birmingham, Cheltenham, Liverpool, and South Shields. The other four – at Bristol, Hull, Sunderland and Wigan – were in arcades, the newest form of shopping centre; and it must have been a landmark in Michael's life when a 10-year lease relating to Wigan, where he had lived until 1893, was signed in July 1899. (The lease, signed on behalf of M & S by a chartered accountant and an architect, survives.)

An even bigger landmark for both Marks and Spencer must have been the year 1904, when they acquired premises at Leeds in the recently opened Cross Arcade, near the present M & S store, to make a new penny bazaar. 'No city in England can boast a more wonderful transformation than that witnessed in Leeds during the last two or three decades', a Leeds Shoppers' Guide claimed in 1909, and 'The centre of Leeds has been practically re-carved and polished'. And the new M & S store was in one of its favourite showplaces.

In general, however, arcade bazaars were to prove less profitable than shops in the main shopping streets, and very soon M & S shops were opened on a wide variety of central sites: for example, at 61/61A Lime Street, Liverpool in 1903; 12 Duke Street, Douglas (Isle of Man) in 1904; 49 Kirkgate, Bradford in 1906; and 7 Castle Street, Bristol in 1907. By then there were no fewer than seven London bazaars, although none was in the central areas. The Brixton bazaar was in the premises of an old Bon Marché shop, and there were other bazaars at Croydon, Kilburn, Kingsland, Islington and Tottenham. New provincial bazaars included Bedford, Blackburn, Grimsby, Harrogate, Newport, Leicester, Luton, Northampton, Preston, Reading, Swansea and Worcester.

There are some details of individual bazaar takings (and outlays) between 1906 and 1910. In 1906 Liverpool, with yearly takings of £9,857, came first in the 'league table', Brixton second with £9,766, Leeds Arcade third with £8,701, and Manchester fourth with £8,459. Other bazaars with yearly takings of over £4,000 were Bristol (£6,242), Newcastle (£5,482), Hull (£4,513), Middlesbrough (£4,064) and Islington, London (£4,055); the Sunderland figure by then was £3,924. The smallest bazaar takings were at Stalybridge, near Manchester (£586); there were five others with takings of less than £1,000.

Mrs Thornton's notebook (*see text*), with details of the first few days' takings at the Sunderland bazaar in November 1895.

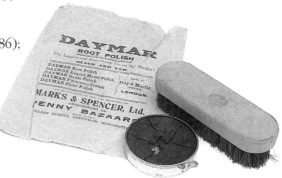

Above: The bazaar at 228 Edgware Road, London, in Edwardian days. Note the distinctive penny symbol above the 'Admission Free' sign.

Main picture: The store in Grainger Market, Newcastle-upon-Tyne, in 1914. The store opened in 1895 and is still in existence today – the last remaining example of these early M & S sites. The paper bag (below) dates from prior to 1901, when the company moved its warehouse from Robert Street to nearby Derby Street, Manchester.

In 1910, the top bazaar was Brixton with £9,367, Liverpool came second with £7,305, Manchester third with £7,238, Hull fourth with £7,015, Bristol fifth with £6,728, and Newcastle sixth with £6,022. Two other bazaars had takings of over £5,000 – Croydon and Newport – and 10 others took more than £4,000, among them a new shop in Bath.

Expansion after 1903 had been on a new financial basis for, on 4 June of that year, when the net profit of the partnership was £6,800, M & S had become a 'company limited by shares', as the Memorandum and Articles of Association put it. It held its first directors' meeting on 12 June – with Michael Marks in the chair and with only a solicitor and an auditor in attendance besides Tom Spencer. The company had the widest possible range of activities: 'To carry on, either in connection with each other or as distinct and separate businesses', the legal jargon read, 'the business or businesses of an Estate Company, Building Contractors, Merchants, Storekeepers, Cooperative Stores, General Supply Society, Furnishing and General Warehousemen, Warehouse Keepers, Publishers, Booksellers, Cabinet Makers, Dealers of and in...', and then a long list of various categories of goods followed – ironmongery, turnery, household fittings and utensils, ornaments, pictures, works of art, stationery and fancy goods, 'commodities of personal and household use', such as hardware, safes, clocks, watches, jewellery, plated goods, glass, leather goods, photo-component parts, musical instruments, and 'articles required for Use, Ornament, Recreation or Amusement'. If this were not comprehensive enough – and certainly some of these items would have cost more than a penny – among the other activities specified were those of drapers, upholsterers, decorators, furniture removers, depositories and manufacturers as well as dealers.

Peddling had been left far behind. Indeed, significant attention was paid throughout the memorandum to property. Article 3(d), for example, permitted the new joint stock company 'to carry on business, whether manufacturing or otherwise, which may seem to the Company capable of being conveniently carried on ... or calculated directly or indirectly to enhance the value of or render more profitable any of the Company's property'. Equally comprehensively, Article 3(f) empowered the Company 'to build, construct, maintain, alter, enlarge, pull down and remove or replace any buildings, factories, mills, offices, works, wharves, roads, railways, machinery, engines, walls, fences, banks, dams, sluices, or watercourses, and to clear sites for the same'.

The financial provisions were basically simple: 'to borrow or raise money in such manner as the Company shall think fit, and in particular by the issue of Debentures or Debenture Stock, perpetual or otherwise' ... or 'also by mortgage, charge or lien'. Yet there was an interesting extra provision set out in Article 3(u): 'to support and subscribe to any charitable or public object, and any institution, society, or club which may be connected with any town or place where the Company carries on business'. Michael Marks set an example here which his successors were all to follow.

The capital of the new company was £30,000 in £1 ordinary shares, of which 14,996 each were allotted to Michael Marks and Thomas Spencer. In addition, one share each went to five other signatories to the memorandum: Agnes Spencer and Hannah Marks; Carl Jacobson, travelling inspector, who may have met Marks before Marks met Spencer; Thomas Spencer junior, warehouseman;

Minutes of a Directors' meeting on 11 January 1905 – one of the last to be attended by Tom Spencer – and Spencer at his farm at Whittington Hill, Lichfield, a month or two before his death in July 1905. Behind him is his wife Agnes.

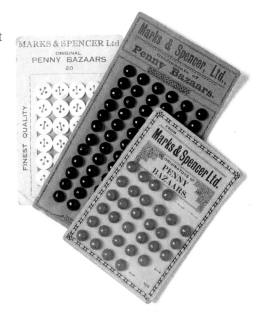

and William Francis Norris, the first M & S male employee. Three shares were not allotted, and remained unallotted until 1906, when for the third time the company's capital was increased, to stand at £33,000.

By then, Tom Spencer had died (on 25 July 1905) and there were 10 new shareholders. Tom had retired from the daily business in the year the company was founded and had gone off to follow his favourite pursuit of farming near Lichfield (Staffordshire). It was a loss to the business, for there was no one who quite took his place. Yet the fact that a limited liability company had been founded was a sign that the original partnership had served its purpose. Continuity had not been broken. M & S was there to stay.

Provision was made in the articles of 1903 that in the event of an increase in capital Michael Marks and Thomas Spencer should have the option of subscribing equally to the whole of any par issue. Now that Tom Spencer was dead, however, there were bound to be family problems. Were the descendants of Michael Marks and Tom Spencer (or their trustees) to enjoy the same rights as the founders? In his will Tom Spencer had stated specifically that it should be lawful for his trustees to 'invest additional capital' in the business of M & S, notwithstanding any of the trusts and provisions in the will, if they thought fit.

Before they were to reveal their intentions, however, new shareholders were named in January 1906 – among them G.R. Kenyon, the auditor; Thomas Williams and Thomas Wilde, warehousemen; and John Littlewood, Abraham Ratner and William McQuillan, stocktakers. Carl Jacobson's holding increased by 301 to the same size of holding as Kenyon's, and that of William Norris, now described as Secretary, by 90.

At the time of the third increase, later in 1906, the 500 new shares allotted to Michael Marks were supplemented on his family's side by 100 allotted to his brother Ephraim, who by then had built up a chain of stores in Scotland, and on the Spencer side by 495 allotted to Tom's widow Agnes and 50 to his son Thomas junior. In June 1902 Tom Spencer had named Isaac Dewhirst as executor of his will along with John Luther Green of Stockton-on-Tees; but in a codicil of July 1905 (a few days before his death) he substituted for Dewhirst his friend William Chapman, handkerchief manufacturer, of Prestwich Park, Manchester. It was a momentous switch of names, for Chapman was to play a crucial role in the early history of the company.

Chapman and Green, the executors of the Spencer estate, got 5 and 50 shares respectively in 1906. Chapman's holding soon rose by 500, he was appointed a director, and within 18 months he would become the most important personality in the business. Laura Cowburn, who had joined Marks and Spencer in 1895, the fourth sales assistant to be appointed, held 10 shares. (She was to marry William McQuillan, and, decades later – in 1959, when at the age of 78 she received a presentation from Lord Marks – she would be described as the 'oldest human link in the business of Marks and Spencer'.) Simon Marks himself did not receive his first allocation of shares until April 1907, when he was 19 years old.

A few months later – and it was a very serious blow for the young Simon and his family – Michael Marks unexpectedly collapsed and died at the age of 48, on 31 December 1907, the last day of the financial year of the business. It had been a successful year, when profits rose from £6,600 to £8,668, and the dividend

Right: Two of the first shareholders – Carl Jacobson ('travelling inspector') and Agnes Spencer, Tom's second wife (from a photograph taken in the 1950s).

Below: The articles of association of the limited-liability company, dated 18 May 1903.

10

We, the several persons whose Names, Addresses, and Descriptions are hereunto subscribed, are desirous of being formed into a Company in pursuance of this Memorandum of Association, and we respectively agree to take the number of Shares in the Capital of the Company set opposite our respective names.

NAMES, ADDRESSES, AND DESCRIPTIONS OF SUBSCRIBERS.	Number of Shares taken by each Subscriber.
Michael Marks 396 Bury New Rd Manchester General Merchant	one
Thomas Spencer, Glenside Prestwich Park Manchester General Merchant	one
Agnes Spencer Spencer Glenside Prestwick Park Manchester (married woman)	one.
Hannah Marks 396 Bury New Road Manchester married woman	one
Carl Jacobson 25 Broughton St Cheetham Manchester travelling inspector	one
Thomas Spencer Jun Glenside Prestwich Pk Manchester Warehouseman.	one.
William Francis Norris School House Road Smedley Manchester Warehouseman	one

Dated the 18 day of May 1903.

Witness to the above Signatures—

Edward J. Usher
52 Corporation St. Manchester
Solicitor

"The Companies Acts, 1862 to 1900."

COMPANY LIMITED BY SHARES.

DUPLICATE

Articles of Association

OF

MARKS AND SPENCER, LIMITED.

PRELIMINARY.

1. The Regulations contained in the Table marked "A," in the First Schedule to The Companies Act, 1862, shall not apply to the Company. *Exclusion of Table A.*

2. In these Articles, unless the context or subject requires a different meaning— *Interpretation Article.*

"The Statutes" shall mean The Companies Acts, 1862 to 1900, and every other Act incorporated therewith.

"The Register" shall mean the Register of Members to be kept as required by Section 25 of The Companies Act, 1862.

"Month" shall mean calendar month.

"Paid up" shall include credited as paid up.

"Secretary" shall include any person appointed to perform the duties of Secretary temporarily.

Words which have a special meaning assigned to them in the Statutes shall have the same meaning in these presents.

Words importing the singular number only, shall include the plural; and the converse shall also apply.

Words importing males shall include females.

Words importing individuals shall include corporations.

paid was 20%. Michael, who had received £400 in salary and £300 in travel expenses, had since 1903 borne the strain of running the new company almost single-handed. It was he who had been responsible for acquiring new premises – six in 1906 alone – for supervising his growing staff, for appointing new people to it, and for travelling inside and outside Britain buying goods for sale. Yet he had never neglected Manchester and his family, and it was said that his funeral attracted the largest crowd in the history of the Jewish community there.

On Michael's death William Chapman became the senior director in the company, Simon Marks attended his first M & S meeting on 22 January 1908, not as a director but (along with his mother and uncle) as a shareholder. At this fascinating point in M & S history the family motive was dominant, for Simon was fortified in his resolve to control the company by what he called 'an obsession' to work for his mother and to accumulate 'a nest egg of £10,000 for her'. He soon realised that, if he were to secure control of M & S, he would, in his own words, have 'a real struggle to do so'. He had no direct experience in retailing and, although he had finished off his Manchester Grammar School education with spells in France and Germany, he had only a limited knowledge of the world. William Chapman, Spencer's masterful executor, was a man of equal determination: born illegitimate and a completely self-made man, he was still young himself – in his late 30s. (He was to die only in 1942 and to leave an estate worth £124,147.) As a boy he had sold newspapers outside Exchange Station, Manchester, and he became a prominent figure in a Manchester mission church, where he taught boys as poor as he himself had been. When, decades later, his handkerchief factory became a juvenile court, his picture was on display and was held up as 'an example to under-privileged youngsters in trouble to show that even the least fortunate could survive through hard work and honesty'.

William Chapman, Spencer's executor (seen here in 1910), became the dominating force in the company's affairs from Michael Marks's death on 31 December 1907 until Simon Marks finally secured effective control of M & S in January 1916.

Article 30 of the company's constitution was simple enough: 'On the death of any member, not being one of several joint holders of shares, the executors or administrators of such deceased member shall be the only persons recognised by the Company as having any title to such shares'. And it was from this article that Chapman derived his power. He was quickly joined in January 1908, however, by Bernhard Steel, Michael Marks's executor, who had close family connections with a building contractor's business.

Clearly the young Simon Marks had to show qualities of character and will, as well as intelligence and imagination, if he was to succeed in securing control of his father's business. Moreover, he could win what he called the 'real struggle' only if he were prepared to buy up at what he considered to be 'a most exorbitant price' some of the non-family shares, shares which when Tom Spencer died had been valued for probate purposes at £3. Simon eight years later had to pay four times as much for them.

Details of shareholdings are often interesting in themselves, for once a company becomes 'a company limited by shares', its base broadens and minority shareholders can find themselves with more influence than they would ever have thought possible. Thomas Spencer junior, who was older than Simon, lacked the sturdy qualities of his father and was soon pushed out of the business picture, although he had taken the place of William Norris as Secretary in January 1906, when Michael Marks was still alive, and had attended the annual meeting along with Chapman. He worked closely with Chapman after Michael's death

Above: The receipt (top), dated 11 February 1914, from Joseph Esterman for the purchase by M & S of the London Penny Bazaar Company. The two lower photographs show the East Ham bazaar of the LPBC in 1911 and after conversion to M & S premises in 1914.

during a turbulent period, lasting from 1908 to 1917, when the board-room history of M & S was more stormy than at any time before or since.

Chapman wished to increase the number of branches of the company – chains of multiple stores were developing rapidly at this time – but in order to do so he needed more capital. In 1908, when there were, as Chapman put it, 'depressed conditions of trade' in the country as a whole, Steel visited Reading, Oxford, Bath and Swindon and prepared reports on prospects there.

Expansion never stopped, whatever the economic circumstances, and in December 1908 Chapman could report record sales during the two weeks preceding and including Christmas. Moreover, in 1909, after new branches had been opened at Hereford, Carlisle, Weston-super-Mare, Hartlepool, and Radcliffe (Manchester), Chapman and Steel made a joint effort to raise extra share capital up to a figure of £100,000.

At this point, differences of approach emerged. Simon Marks, anxious to protect his controlling family interest, saw the long-term implications of this move (a lessening of his family's proportion of the total shares) and sought to delay it; and although a motion proposed by Steel and seconded by Ephraim Marks recommending an increase in company capital to £66,000 by the creation of 33,000 new shares was carried unanimously in February 1911, it was never put into effect. On the back of a letter there are historically fascinating scribbled (and undated) pencil notes by Simon Marks addressed to Chapman objecting to the issue of new shares 'with the probable allocation of some to yourself' and adding 'I trust that after considering the views expressed by me you will see your way clear to act in accordance with such views particularly having regard to the fact that my family & self are the persons whose interests are at stake'. Marks objected also to Chapman and Steel calling themselves 'Managing Directors'.

The date was obviously some time in 1911 and, very soon afterwards, Chapman and Steel parted company after disagreements about the main business of board meetings, property transactions and management – Brighton, Nottingham, King's Lynn and Maidstone were among the locations where there had been trouble about overcharging – in which Steel, through relatives in the contracting business, had been directly involved. Steel submitted his resignation, nominally on grounds of health, 'a cause for great anxiety', on 7 September 1912. He did not die until 1929.

Arguments about direction of the company revealed a difference of outlook between the able but essentially cautious Chapman, who was uneasy about 'over-buying stock' (a subject first raised at a board meeting in 1908), and Marks, who considered that active buying was indispensable. There were arguments, too, about the composition of the board and voting rights. When, for example, at the Annual Ordinary General Meeting in February 1913 Simon Marks had proposed the election as a director of Alexander Isaacs, a trustee under his father's will, four votes had been cast in favour and four against, and in a poll called for by Marks the proposal had been carried by 16,782 votes to 16,218. Yet Chapman, supported by the company's solicitor, who was also his personal solicitor, blocked the way, objecting to some of the proxies – as did Simon Marks himself – and laying down that the election of a new director required to be authorised by a special resolution.

In the meantime, the value of the enterprise increased so substantially that the prospect of controlling it became more and more tempting. Indeed, during the six years following Michael's death, turnover increased from £177,600 to £392,600 and profits from £8,000 to £30,000, and these in face of increasing competition: in particular, Woolworth's crossed the Atlantic, opening its first store in Liverpool on 5 November 1909, 60,000 people visiting the store on that and the following day.

There are no references to the opening in the M & S board minutes, but throughout 1909 there was considerable discussion about repainting and redecoration of the bazaars – at Gloucester there was a thorough 'overhauling', at Grimsby there was 'total remodelling' – and about better lighting inside and the possibility of heating (though the difficulties of heating shops with open fronting was apparent). There was even talk of establishing penny bazaars in Belgium.

In 1911 M & S acquired for £1,565 the bankrupt Arcadia Bazaar Company, a chain of bazaars in the London area. A year later, it secured leases and fittings of four penny bazaars – at Colchester, Great Yarmouth, Southampton, Swindon – and a warehouse in Adelina Grove, near the Mile End Road, belonging to the London Penny Bazaar Company. This last was owned by the brothers Joseph and Louis Esterman, who had put in a bid for the Arcadia Bazaar Company against M & S in 1911. There were also discussions with the Peacock Bazaar Company in 1912. In July 1913, after Joseph Esterman had attended a meeting of the board and there had been secret negotiations, not recorded in detail, M & S obtained for £15,000 in cash as a going concern the whole of the LPBC property.

A third of all the M & S branches were now in the London area – among them Barking, East Ham, Fulham, Hackney, Hammersmith, Holloway, Islington, Peckham, Southwark, Tooting, Walthamstow and Woolwich – so that London was beginning to take the place of Manchester as the main centre of the company's retail business. Further warehouses were opened in Birmingham and London. They supplemented Derby Street, Manchester, although Derby Street remained the registered office of the company until 1924.

Indeed, whatever differences there were behind the scenes, there was obvious continuity of management, and not even the outbreak of war could disrupt it. In August 1914 the Directors' Minutes read, one week after war was declared, 'In consequence of the war crisis, the conducting of business affairs in the future was well considered', and it was resolved that 'business for the present be carried on as usual'. There was only one new sign of the times. In October 1914, the firm's Studebaker car was offered for sale to the *Daily Sketch* fund, 'the proceeds to go to providing comforts for the soldiers or relief of their dependants'.

Nevertheless, the struggle for control was only in abeyance, and in 1915 Chapman once again blocked a Marks proposal, this time to elect Alexander Isaacs and Israel Sieff to the board: it was made at a tense Extraordinary General Meeting in November 1915, when Hannah Marks, Ephraim Marks and Agnes Spencer were among those present. Chapman declared on this occasion that such a resolution required a three-to-one majority and that, as the Spencer trustees objected to the resolution, it would be 'useless to put it to the meeting'. Simon disputed his ruling, but on a show of hands Simon's resolution was defeated by 8 votes to 5. In a subsequent poll, however, there were 16,782 in

East Ham, continued: construction (top) of a new store in February 1929 and (centre) soon after its opening in the following August; and (bottom) the newly built East Ham store in September 1964.

favour of Simon's resolution and 16,218 against – but that did not constitute a three-to-one majority.

Chapman followed up this victory by proposing at the next meeting of the directors that in future the quorum for directors should be two, giving as his reason Marks's failure to attend recent board meetings. He went on, at the same meeting, also to have carried a proposal to add a director of his choosing, the company's first male employee, William Norris, to the board.

The future of M & S was once more in the balance, although Chapman now felt himself in a strong enough position to make a concession, and he stated that he was willing to admit Israel Sieff to the board in the same way as Norris had been admitted. He would still, of course, have been left with a majority on the board.

There was, in fact, no room for lasting compromise, although the quorum was raised to three again in December 1915, and Sieff joined the board (with Isaacs) in the same month, when he attended his first board meeting. The Secretary was finding it increasingly difficult in these circumstances to keep minutes which would command general assent, and Simon Marks reached the decision to abandon further talk and go to law. The result was a complete victory for him. In Court of Chancery in December 1915, before Mr Justice Peterson, it was determined that the election of Sieff and Isaacs by a simple majority of voting shares was valid, as was the power of a general meeting to increase the number of directors; and when Chapman appealed, the judgement was upheld with the minimum of delay by Lord Justice Warrington in January 1916.

This was the end of the beginning of the story of M & S. Simon Marks took the chair for the first time in February 1916 and, although Chapman returned to it for several meetings in the early months of 1916, in August 1916 Simon Marks was formally voted to the chair, and in June 1917 Chapman and Thomas Spencer junior, who had taken little part recently in the management of the company (and who had been invited to resign in August 1916), formally retired from the board. Neither of them was present on this occasion. John Luther Green and Alfred Davis were subsequently appointed to represent the Spencer interest, while Marks and Sieff, both in their 29th year, formed what was in effect a new partnership into whose hands the future of M & S passed.

It was ironical that these dramatic events, which few of M & S's customers knew anything about, took place in the most difficult months of the First World War, when bloody battles were being fought in France and when the M & S penny bazaars in Britain were emptier of goods than they had been since the foundation of the business. Yet in 1915, when the board-room battles reached their climax, a 50% dividend was paid, one of the highest in the company's history, and turnover was more than £400,000. By then there were 145 branches, only 10 of them in market halls. No less than 56 were in London and the London area. Four store properties were owned freehold. The first of them was at Portsmouth and had cost £3,755 in 1909; the second was at Sunderland, the third at Brighton, and the fourth at Reading.

Business operations had inevitably deteriorated as the First World War dragged on and put paid to the original expectations of 'Business as Usual', as the slogan put it. The government was slow to develop an apparatus of control, but M & S's relations with most suppliers were immediately jeopardised or even broken (particularly in the case of overseas supplies), transport was difficult, production

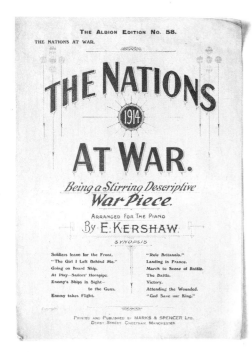

was restricted, prices rose, heavier stocks had to be carried, and it proved impossible to maintain the penny-price policy on which the business had been built. Goods, not customers, dictated policies, for like any retail concern M & S had to buy and sell whatever goods were obtainable at whatever prices were set for them. Moreover, M & S had to borrow money, which it had never had to do since the company was formed in 1903. By August 1916, a few months after the law case, bank loans and overdrafts amounted to £57,000, and by the middle of 1918 they had reached £75,000. Profits, too, fell for the first time, and, notwithstanding inflation, would be lower in money terms (after tax) at the end of the war than they had been at the beginning.

Meanwhile, in May 1917 Simon, who had borne the brunt of the work of the business, was called away from shopkeeping to be a gunner in the army, although very soon his duties would be of a different and quite exceptional kind. Indeed, they were greatly to influence the shape of his later life as Chairman of the company as well as citizen. At first he served in a barracks at Preston – and it was possible to hold board meetings there, which he chaired in uniform. Later in 1917 the Prime Minister, Arthur Balfour, arranged for his demobilization so that he could become secretary of the Palestine commission set up to support Dr Chaim Weizmann and his Zionist organisation. Israel Sieff was already involved in it as Weizmann's personal assistant. The links forged then were to survive the war and to gain in historic importance. When Marks and Sieff died, some of the most eloquent tributes to them came from the new state of Israel, of which Weizmann had dreamed and of which he became the first President in 1948.

Marks and Sieff came to know Weizmann in Manchester when he was fashioning the Zionist movement. Weizmann was to influence future M & S policies very directly, for it was he, as a brilliant scientist (he lectured in chemistry at Manchester University), who explained to Marks and Sieff the part that technology could and should play in a retail business. It was a result of his stimulus that M & S became involved in technology to an extent that other retailers could not always understand.

That was in the future. Meanwhile, Sieff was granted leave of absence 'in consequence of the important duties he has undertaken', and Alexander Isaacs and John Luther Green were persuaded to become full-time directors, the former becoming acting Vice-Chairman in June 1918. A month later, Simon Marks, 'after a few well-chosen words', presented William Norris with a cheque for £200 and a gold watch suitably inscribed in recognition of 25 years service. Despite all the 'interruptions' of the war – as they were seen at the time – M & S was honouring long service, as it always was to do, while laying the foundation for a new phase in its history.

Below: Patriotic handkerchief and (opposite page) stirring sheet music were typical M & S lines during the First World War.

Below, left: Simon Marks in gunner's uniform in July 1917. For a few months that year he held board meetings at a hotel near his barracks in Preston.

ARCHITECT'S MODEL AND ELEVATION FOR STORES IN THE 1930s

HOW TO GROW

MARKS & SPENCER LTD.
REGISTERED OFFICES
DERBY STREET.
CHEETHAM
MANCHESTER

In the first post-war year, 1919, M & S turnover was £550,000; 20 years later, in 1939, it was £23,448,000. In that year there were 234 stores and over 17,000 employees. In 1924 the head office of the company had been transferred from Manchester to Friendly House, 21-3 Chiswell Street, London, EC1. New premises, also in Chiswell Street, were acquired and rebuilt as Michael House at a cost of £29,000 and were opened in 1928; and in 1931 Michael House moved to 72-82 Baker Street. M & S was now a nationwide organisation with branches in London, the rest of England, Scotland and Wales, and when war broke out in 1939 plans were ready for the construction of a new central office building.

During these inter-war years, when the numbers of small retailers were falling and when multiple stores and department stores were increasing in size and in share of the market, the M & S store, looking very different from the old penny bazaar, became a major feature of the local scene in all of England's larger shopping centres. It was sometimes next to and often opposite Woolworth's, and as its main neighbours it usually had multiple-shop branches, many of them newly established companies with very mixed fortunes. One thing that Woolworth's and M & S had in common – and they were both successes – was that they positively welcomed people going inside, even if they did not buy. 'The moment you go into an English shop', Frank Woolworth had written after his first visit to Europe in 1900, 'you are expected to buy, and to have made your choice from the window. They give you an icy stare if you follow the American custom of just going to look around'.

There were no icy stares in either Woolworth's or M & S and, although the two stores were to follow quite different patterns of development, they were alike, too, in their desire to make their premises tempting. Indeed, H. Pasmardjian in his valuable *The Department Store – Its Origin, Evolution & Economics* (1954) pointed out how during the 1920s and 1930s M & S gave rise 'to an entirely new form of business, located half way between the unit price store and the department store and which, penetrating deeply into the assortment of department stores', made inroads upon their trade.

Prices still mattered to M & S customers but, as was pointed out in one of the surprisingly few books on retailing published at the time, Dorothea Braithwaite and S.P. Dobbs' *Distribution of Consumable Goods* (1932), 'palatial premises, numerous and well-trained shop-assistants, a large choice of goods and similar articles attract the public more successfully than would a slight price difference'. It was not just that large-scale retailing was supplanting (though not destroying) small-scale retailing: shops, like cinemas, were part of a new urban landscape, and the very place of retailing in society was changing too. At the end of the First World War, 10% of Britain's workers were employed in the distributive trades: on the outbreak of the Second World War the figure was 13%. This was not just replacement. It was growth.

It would not have been easy to forecast the scale of this development

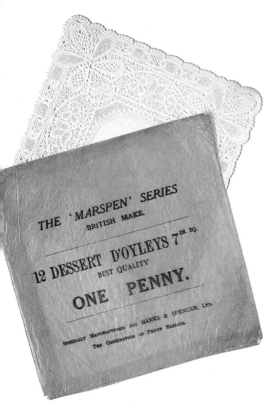

immediately after the First World War. Indeed, in 1921, 1922 and 1923 problems at M & S loomed as large as opportunities. One of the most serious of them was business loss at a number of old, well-established M & S centres. It was decided in consequence in June 1923, for instance, to close down Bolton, Cardiff and Wakefield market stalls.

The other serious problems were finding finance for new development and replanning merchandising policy. In 1919 the company had acquired 13 freehold store properties and in 1920 another 11, but many of these were mortgaged from the start and there were worrying bank overdrafts. As for merchandising, how could M & S develop logically and consistently in the future given that the penny limit set before the war could no longer work? 'We continued to sell goods at a wide range of prices', Simon Marks wrote later, 'which presented a confusing picture to the customer, and I came to the conclusion that a simpler price structure was essential'.

Problems were transformed into opportunities after M & S was converted into a public company in 1926. Indeed, two years before that Simon Marks had begun to find answers both to the financial problem and to the retailing problem when he visited the United States, the first of many visits across the Atlantic. He has described vividly and succinctly in his own brief account of M & S history what happened as a result of his American visit:

> Having assumed control of the private Company, I was free to face up to its problems. Woolworth's had been making extraordinary progress and were rapidly developing throughout the country. They had become a household word, a great commercial institution. We had marked time and could report no change since the days of my father, other than a few more branches.
>
> I was conscious of my own shortcomings and ignorance. I had never worked

Below: M & S in Cardiff – the super-store (left) under construction in June 1932 just before its opening, and (right) the market stall, seen here in 1901.

in a shop. I had no training in the business, other than that which I was to acquire by trial and error. I felt that somehow I had to expand my experience, learn from other people how to face up to the competition from this commercial giant whose red signs were beginning to dominate the main shopping streets of Great Britain.

A distant relative from New York, Herman Germain, happened to be in London on business. I told him of my anxieties – how did others in the United States counter this opposition? Could other businesses live side by side and still prosper? I did not then realise how open, helpful and generous American businessmen were in showing strangers how they operated. They seemed to have no secrets from one another – so different in England, where everybody seems to have secrets from everybody else....

It was about my first serious lesson in the chain-store art. I learned the value of more imposing, commodious premises, modern methods of administration and the statistical control of stocks in relation to sales. I learned that new accounting machines could help to reduce the time to find the necessary information to hours instead of weeks. There was no doubt that these methods of control were to help us in the speedy development of our business. Hitherto, we had always been behindhand in our information, which was a formidable handicap in our buying. I learned the value of counter footage, that is, that each counter foot of space had to pay wages, rent, overhead expenses, and earn a profit. There could be no blind spots on the counters insofar as goods were concerned. This meant a much more exhaustive study of the goods we were selling and the needs of the public. It meant that the staff who were operating with me had to be re-directed and re-trained. It meant new people, new faces.

America showed the way as far as the answers to all Marks's strictly retailing questions were concerned. 'The policy we should follow was now clear', he recalled years later. 'Nothing over 5s, an extensive programme of enlarging and improving our shops, and the introduction of shelf-stock checking lists which controlled the production and flow of goods from factory to shops. This is still the basis of our stock control'.

How much had to be done to improve the properties was set out in a report and valuation of freehold and leasehold properties prepared by Messrs Hillier, Parker, May & Rowden. Shop-fronts, it pointed out, varied considerably, though those in newly acquired properties were 'of excellent design and particularly well suited for business'. In some of the old stores the construction inside in plain wood was 'somewhat rough'. The Chiswell Street headquarters themselves, close to Liverpool Street station, were described as 'well maintained and in an excellent state of repair'. Fortunately for M & S, locations were right 'in the majority of instances', the report suggested, 'and your branches occupy the most sought-after retail trading spots in their respective districts'.

The primary purpose behind the setting up of a new public company was not managerial but financial – to raise additional funds. In 1926, under the auspices of the Industrial Finance and Investment Corporation, associated with the Prudential Assurance Company, the old company was voluntarily liquidated – William Chapman attended its last meeting – and the new public company was created.

Top: The company's headquarters and warehouse in Derby Street; the building was later taken over by the now defunct national daily, *News Chronicle*.

Bottom: The headquarters office in Chiswell Street, London, EC1, where the company moved in 1924.

Contrasting styles in stores: above, Kilburn bazaar in 1918; above right, Portsmouth bazaar during the First World War, when the penny-price policy was abandoned; below right, London Road, Croydon in 1906 – one of the few M & S stores at that time to take £100 a week.

The institutional support of the Prudential Assurance Company was essential at this point in the history of M & S, although later shareholders were to be attracted from almost as many sections of society as M & S customers. Sir George May, the influential Secretary of the Prudential, looked very carefully at the accounts and prepared 'a chart as to the development of the business' which proved extraordinarily accurate, while Simon Marks was willing at every stage to meet him more than half way in order to get the deal through as expeditiously as possible.

Questions of valuation and capital were crucial in the negotiations, as was the disposal of the specific Spencer interests, although Tom Spencer's widow Agnes retained hers. Yet the future hinged more on business acumen than on financial accommodation. The main Prudential negotiator, Lionel Fraser, noted this in his autobiography *All To the Good* (1963). 'We were very proud of our early connection with M & S', he wrote then. 'Even in those days, it was obvious to us that this concern had genius behind it'.

The financial accommodation proved straightforward once an arrangement had been reached with the Prudential. The public company, which was then operating 135 shops and stores, had an initial capital of 1 million ordinary shares of 10s each, £330,000 of which were issued, and 350,000 cumulative participating preference shares of £1. It was hoped that thereafter there would be 'an ample margin of working capital for ... the programme of development'; in fact, more funds had to be acquired in 1929, 1930, and 1934 in order to implement an ambitious improvement, replacement and multiplication programme.

Thereafter, ploughed-back profits were the main source of finance, supported by debentures. By 1930 approximately four-fifths of the new company's assets consisted of freehold and leasehold properties; and by 1937, 10 years after the public company was launched (and profits had increased from £75,000 to £1,430,000), £7,250,000 out of the £8 million of new capital raised had been invested in properties.

Between 1931 and 1935, 129 new stores were built or rebuilt, and between 1936 and 1939 a further 33. Indeed, by 1939 well over half of M & S's 234 stores had been built or rebuilt by the company. The cost of rebuilding and modernising a store by that date might be as much as £50,000, as compared with £400 or £500 for opening and equipping a new shop in the mid-1920s.

On the eve of the Second World War Simon Marks, surveying the remarkable progress of M & S during the previous 13 years, laid more emphasis on the replacement of old premises by new and larger stores than on increasing the number of stores. 'An M & S store of today', he told his shareholders, 'is, in size, equipment and appearance, a very different institution from what it was even as recently as two or three years ago'. The first new 'super-stores' of the 1920s fully to represent the policy change had been at Birkenhead and Blackpool, both of which were opened in 1923. They each had more than double the frontage of the old penny bazaars and far greater depth. They had plate-glass windows (Blackpool still retained the word 'Bazaar' on them), long wide counters, and greatly improved lighting. A year later, a distinctive green and gold facia, contrasting with Woolworth's red, was introduced. And all the time M & S were looking for the best urban sites.

The inter-war approach at its most dynamic was reflected in the description in a

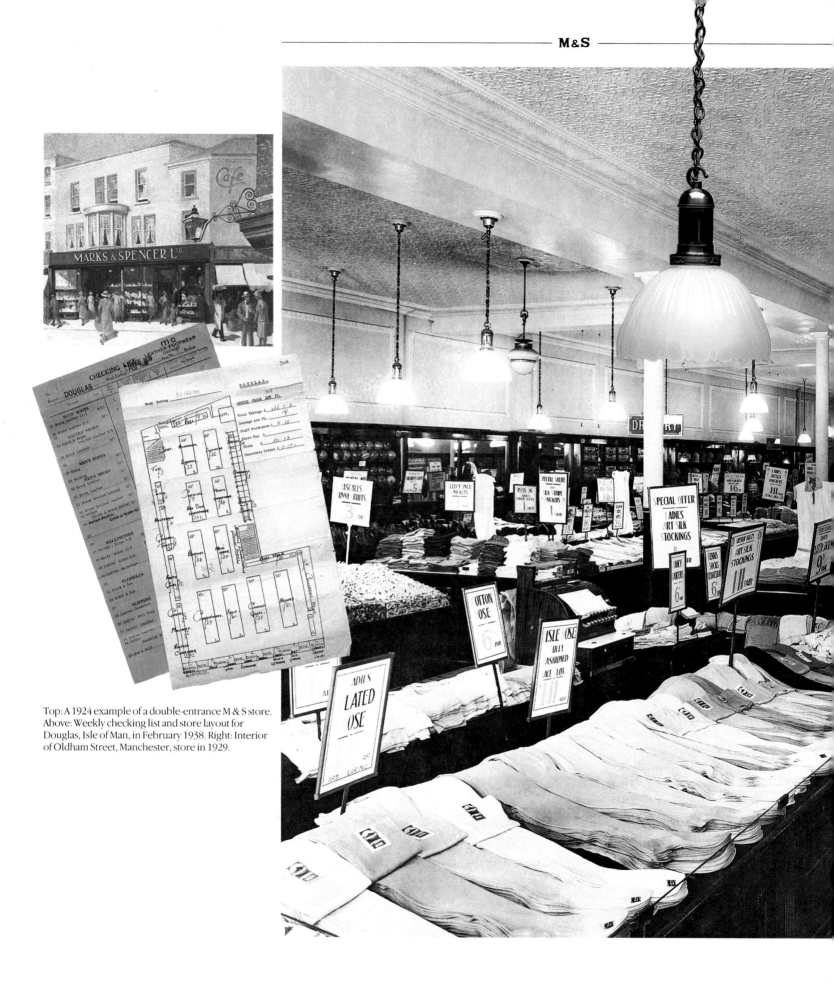

Top: A 1924 example of a double-entrance M & S store. Above: Weekly checking list and store layout for Douglas, Isle of Man, in February 1938. Right: Interior of Oldham Street, Manchester, store in 1929.

Below: Newspaper advertisement announcing the opening of the store in Mansfield in July 1938.

Bottom: Super-store, 1935: the neo-classical idiom.

Top: Local paper announcement of M & S's move to a new super-store at Chatham in September 1934.

local newspaper of the opening of the 'mammoth' M & S store in Chatham (Kent) in September 1934 under the headline 'A Business That Is a Science'. 'In thirteen weeks', the reporter noted, 'an army of workmen have demolished older buildings, set back a frontage line of sixty-three feet and...erected model business premises in which nearly eighty local girls will find employment'. The public would be 'amazed at the wonderful organisation which has produced such a store. Everything is in readiness, and big business is bound to succeed'.

It was – given the drive and the underlying philosophy of M & S. Yet the company never grew on the basis of a formula. 'Our development has not been mechanical', Simon Marks insisted, 'not the mere adding of unit to unit. It has been organic, shaped by the need to adapt ourselves to the changes which were taking place'.

The Prudential negotiator in 1926 recognised this when he wrote, long after the negotiations were over, 'Somebody once called Lord Marks "the Artist of the Penny Bazaars". Certainly he has gone very far since we acted for him in his first call for money from the public. It has been a story of dynamic leadership, of remarkable enterprise and a unique flexibility of vision. A success which has been created, extraordinarily enough, without any advertising, the reputation and the quality of M & S goods being passed by word of mouth'.

The last point was an important one to make. Some historians have referred to the inter-war change in retailing as the beginnings of the growth of 'admass', of a consumer society activated by advertising. In fact M & S advertising was always on a strictly limited scale. The goods and the services spoke for themselves.

Immediately after the formation of the public company, Israel Sieff became a full-time director and Vice-Chairman of an enlarged board, prompting Simon to write that he felt that he had at last secured 'that intelligent co-operation which is essential if we are to get the uttermost out of our business'. Norman Laski and, later, Harry Sacher, both of whom gave invaluable moral and financial support on the eve of the founding of the company, support which Simon described as 'manna from heaven', joined the board too.

In the new M & S prospectus of 1926 it had been stressed that 'The additional capital resulting from the present sale of Preference Shares will provide for the construction and equipment of further "super stores" having an extensive area and scope for the display of goods upon the most modern principles of merchandising'.

When M & S capital was further increased to £1,200,000 in 1929, work on 22 stores was already in the pipeline. Steps were also being taken to find a site for a new store in the West End of London, and 500,000 new A shares of 10s each were authorised. (One new A share was issued free to existing shareholders for every 10 shares held.)

The new A shares carried no voting rights. Management was thus kept firmly separate from the control of those shareholders. It was not until 1966 that this position was changed on the initiative of the new Chairman, Israel Sieff, who felt that by that time the granting of voting rights was 'in tune with the enlightened policy which governs our business'.

The Prudential stake was of major financial importance to M & S before 1939.

Above all else it ensured easy access to capital. Thus when in 1930, after national economic conditions had deteriorated, a further £1 million of 7% M & S preference shares and £1 million of debenture stock at 6% were issued, it was the Prudential Assurance Company which took over the whole of the latter, secured by a first specific mortgage. Co-operative stores at this time, looking at the finance and forgetting what was going on in the stores, were inclined to treat M & S as a magnificent piece of City-backed investment in real estate.

The last pre-war M & S appeal to the public was in 1934, when there were the first signs of recovery from the economic depression, a depression which had done nothing to hold back the expansion of M & S. In that year 2,200,000 additional 5s A shares were authorised for issue to shareholders at £1 a share, and the nominal capital of the company was raised to £3,050,000.

Throughout both the depression years and the years of limited recovery, both turnover and profit always rose annually (*see table at right*).

It is significant that the biggest annual numerical increase in turnover was achieved in 1938, a year of recession when there was a slight upturn in unemployment. Living standards were improving, and it was that which affected M & S most.

It is interesting to compare the 'league table' of store takings in 1930 (when conditions were deeply depressed) and 1935 (when there were signs of improvement). In a week in March 1930 the leading stores in order were Nottingham, Woolwich, Birmingham, Oldham Street (Manchester), Kilburn (where a new London store had been opened in 1929), Bristol, York (where store alterations had just been completed), Liverpool, Sheffield, Portsmouth, Southport, and Glasgow (Argyll Street – a store purchased from Ephraim Marks and Company in 1919). And for a similar period in 1935 Marble Arch in London (opened in November 1930) came first, Glasgow (now a new store, also in Argyll Street) second, Birmingham third, and Cardiff fourth.

Wigan had a new M & S store in October 1931, as did Halifax, Rotherham and Rochdale in 1933, the worst year of the depression. For M & S the record of success in the early 1930s was impressive enough for further bonus shares to be issued to shareholders every year and for the company's capital to stand at £3,950,000 when the Second World War began.

M & S was obviously an excellent investment in difficult times, as it was to prove an excellent investment later in good times. Yet the reasons require fuller explanation. First, and most important, there was growing demand for the articles on sale in its new super-stores. The main reason for this was that, despite unemployment, the real wages of people still in work rose even during the worst depression years. Consequently the number of customers grew. Second, there were changes of taste. Customers were better educated, more aware of quality and of fashion. Third, the production of consumer goods was becoming more sophisticated: there was unprecedented scientific and technological progress in this field, and every store was treated as a laboratory in which the demands of the public could be tested day by day, even minute by minute.

These conditions set the terms for market expansion and influenced the range of goods and their layout in the new stores. Before 1914 store-building had posed many difficulties. Now a single Building Department dealt with architects,

YEAR	TURNOVER £000	PROFIT BEFORE TAX £000	PROFIT AFTER TAX £000
1929	2,493	235	181
1930	3,605	335	261
1931	5,360	476	359
1932	6,936	670	476
1933	8,356	817	572
1934	10,138	976	690
1935	11,398	1,087	805
1936	14,269	1,264	939
1937	16,284	1,433	1,015
1938	20,015	1,577	1,028
1939	23,448	1,757	1,127

Annual turnover and profit in the Depression and post-Depression years.

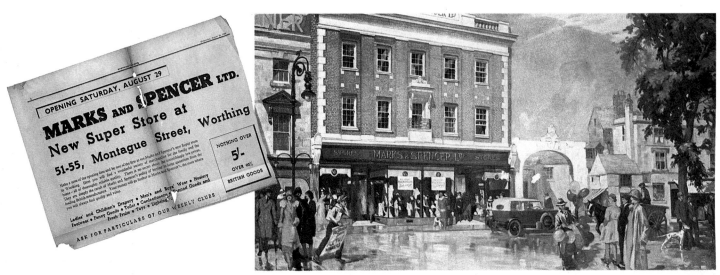

The company undertook an enormously ambitious building programme in the 1920s and 1930s: by the outbreak of the Second World War in 1939 there were no fewer than 237 stores. The paintings on this page exemplify the architectural styles of that period. Top: A neo-Georgian façade of 1935, designed to blend with neighbouring 18th century buildings. Centre: A typical super-store elevation of the early 1930s. Bottom: Design for an island site in Nottingham in 1939.

engineers and surveyors, and a single contracting firm, Bovis, was appointed in 1926. The first store for which the firm contracted was at Wood Green (London), and this was quickly followed by one at Gravesend. Thereafter M & S could maintain an experienced work-force and secure advantages of bulk purchase and continuity of operation. In 1931 lease arrangements were standardised too and wherever possible leases were enfranchised.

By later standards the first new stores were modest – with a simple internal steel framework within load-bearing external walls supporting a timber-constructed floor and roof slabs and an asphalt roof. The architect, P. Hickey, who carried out his first professional job for M & S in 1922, writing years later, noted that the total cost of some of them was about the same as that of the electrical installation in the new stores of the 1950s. By earlier M & S standards, however, they were highly advanced, and they allowed for further improvement, particularly in stock and staff areas and in engineering services.

It was the ambition of M & S that it should so display its merchandise to the public that it came as near as possible to the way it would look in daylight – and to use the most immediately informative price tickets, a new development which brightened the stores as well as helped the customers. A small printing department, which was set up on the fifth floor of Michael House in 1931 – with a staff of two, two Multigraph machines, and a small hand-operated guillotine – was very quickly expanded. A year later it had doubled in size, and it was soon moved to Mile End, in east London, where by 1939 staff numbers had risen to 28. They printed price tags, forms, instructions and reports. The house journal *Sparks*, which first appeared in 1934, was a testimony, too, to the increasingly articulate concern for 'welfare' in the M & S business, a regular theme of articles in the journal and the theme of later chapters in this book. Growth, it was always recognised, depended on a lively as well as a contented staff. In 1937 J.H. Morgan, the editor of *Sparks*, writing on the subject of welfare, noted that for more than 25 years the policy of the directors had 'progressed with, and was very often in advance of, the times, otherwise the business would not have developed into the vast and efficient organisation it is today'. What would he have said if he could have looked on 40 years to 1977? 'Being in advance' in 1937 meant looking forward into the kind of future which was not to be realised until 20 years later.

It was Simon Marks who found the right words for the period in 1936, when the public company was 10 years old. 'Goods and services once regarded as luxuries', he told shareholders then, 'have become conventional comforts and are now almost decreed necessities. A fundamental change in people's habits has been brought about. Millions are enjoying a substantially higher standard of living. To this substantial rise in the standard of living our Company claims to have made a definite contribution'.

Earlier in his speech he had amplified his statement in what was in effect a 10-year general assessment, social as well as economic:

Improvements in the efficiency of production, brought by inventions, scientific technique and more rational administration, enable us to produce constantly increasing quantities of goods at lower prices, and to extend the range of commodities manufactured. But they can only be produced if distribution is adequately organised to deal with their sale and the necessary

Opposite page and above: Advertisements for super-store openings in 1936.

services attendant upon their use. Production and distribution are intimately associated, and, if properly coordinated, react on each other advantageously. But efficient distribution is not a static conception. It involves constant alertness and study of the changing habits, desires and tastes of the community. The consumer's choice depends on his outlook, his income and his desire to be in fashion. The study of these changing demands is the task of the distributor, who must be ready to adapt himself to the moods of the market and to interpret them to the manufacturers.

The implications of this assessment, which is central to this book, are dealt with more fully in the next three chapters, but before the different strands are traced it is essential to note that Marks's assessment was very much a Marks/Sieff assessment. Indeed, between 1926 and 1936 the initials M & S had come to stand for Marks and Sieff. Their almost telepathic relationship was the key to growth and to the form growth took.

Israel Sieff has given his own account of these 10 years in a chapter in his *Memoirs* (1970) entitled 'Simon Reshapes Marks and Spencer', in which he describes how his own 'mission' within the business was 'to lead the campaign for increased direct dealing with the textiles manufacturer'. Yet he also explains that his was far more than a 'single-mission' task. He thought he had come for only a year: he was to stay on to succeed Simon as Chairman.

'We saw, not through visionary idealists' clouds', Israel Sieff wrote of his partnership with Marks, 'but from practical results in days of high competition

The site at 448-450 Brixton Road, London, before and during conversion in autumn 1931.

that production and distribution could become a cooperative process making a positive palpable contribution to the common good'. 'Our discussions, day in and day out, week in and week out', wrote Marks, '…resulted in our evolving a policy and a philosophical outlook on business and life which are the foundations of our business'.

The visible culmination of the pre-war period of M & S expansion was the building of the Pantheon store, 'London's Finest Variety Store', at 178 Oxford Street, erected in 28½ weeks. It was opened in October 1938, and although it was advertised (a rare phenomenon) in the London evening newspapers as offering 'reliable merchandise at prices which the public can afford to pay', it introduced into M & S retailing the full flavour of the upper-income-bracket department store. 'This was the store to out-store all stores', P. Hickey wrote in 1954, 'and the amounts involved in the acquisition of the site and the building were…by comparison with the stores which had already been erected, quite astronomical'.

Hickey was writing during the biggest and most lively period of expansion in the history of M & S, although there are now many new stores which make the 1938 Pantheon look like a historic building belonging very much to its period. Indeed, a record of development of store fittings and equipment, published in 1964, was to begin with a picture of a 1933 store to which the almost archaeological caption read: 'Dark mahogany counters. Heavy ornamentation. Sloping wood boards for textiles. No space for sweeping under. Height of counter 3′ 1″. Height of glass 7″. Note wooden floor. Tungsten lighting using Moonstone shades with chain suspension. Large fitting in foreground is emergency gas light'.

The appearance of stores was to change – and had to change – with the times and with the products on sale. These are described in later chapters, as is the economic performance of the post-war years. Already, however, by 1939 M & S had provided its own answers to the question 'how to grow?'. And it survived its biggest test in 1964 with the death of Simon Marks – in harness, in his office – who had done so much to make it grow. The succession was maintained – first, as he would always have wished, in the hands of his closest friend, Israel Sieff, from 1964 to 1967, then of Israel's brother, J. Edward Sieff, from 1967 to 1972, and then of Israel's son, Marcus Sieff, who had joined M & S in 1935 and had been Vice-Chairman since 1965.

Already in 1966, when Israel Sieff was Chairman, M & S was earning a net profit per employee of £1,146 and £8 15s of profit per square foot of selling space. And its average net profit per store was £128,000 as against £35,000 for a Woolworth's store. It was clear by then that it was not the number of stores as such which counted as far as total performance was concerned, but selling space and its profitability and (of course) what was being sold in it. Marble Arch, a 'flagship store', by 1980 had 103,300 square feet of store space (with more than 1,400 staff), and between then and 1984 total M & S floor space throughout the country rose from 6,374,000 square feet to 6,971,000 square feet – with another 2,220,000 square feet in Canada and 262,000 square feet in continental Europe. And by 1984 there were 262 stores in the United Kingdom; in Canada there were 213 stores and in Europe 9.

The quest to grow, therefore, had led M & S both across the Atlantic and across the Channel. Not content with one nation of customers, it was seeking to win over other nations too.

The Pantheon, Oxford Street, London had enjoyed various incarnations before it was opened as an M & S super-store in October 1938. The playbill dates from exactly a century and a quarter earlier; the photograph was taken in the first decade of the present century, when the building was the headquarters of Messrs W. & A. Gilbey, the wine and spirit firm.

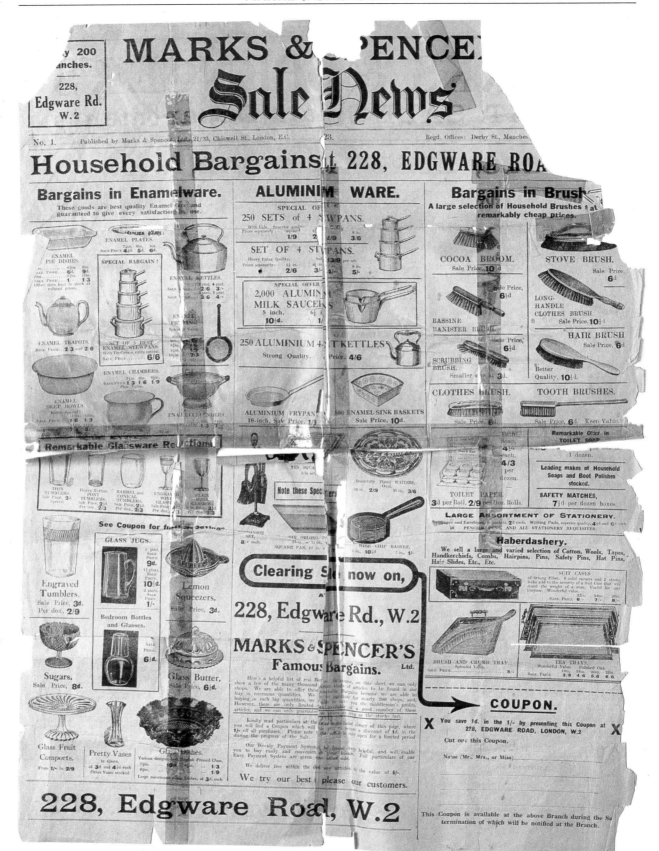

A *SALE NEWS* PUBLISHED BY THE EDGWARE ROAD, LONDON, STORE IN 1923

WHAT TO SELL

The first articles that Michael Marks sold on his stalls were all items which he could acquire conveniently and cheaply and dispose of quickly. He had strictly limited choice and he could not hold much by way of stock. The first line with which he is said to have been successful was reels of cotton. He bought them from Dewhirst at 11 shillings a gross and sold them at a penny each.

The penny policy, well established by the time Spencer joined Marks as partner in 1894, set the framework for the selling policies of M & S until 1914, and customers bought exactly the same range of goods in each store, with the exception of a few stores, like Cheltenham, which had 4½d and 10½d limits, and Carlisle and Kingsland (London), which had 6d departments.

The Victorian penny, however, was quite a different coin from today's penny. Even by 1914 and the outbreak of the First World War, a penny would buy rather less, particularly of food, than it had done in 1884. The real value of the penny has to be related, of course, to the incomes of M & S customers, and there is a further complication in making comparisons across time. The introduction of decimal coinage in 1970 changed all the terms of reference. For centuries there had been 12 pennies in a shilling. There were also 20 shillings to the £, and 4 farthings to every penny. Both farthings and halfpennies were coins in general use. For the rich they were change: for the poor they were very serious coins indeed. And Michael Marks himself, like Tom Spencer, had counted every farthing. When the London, City & Midland Bank Ltd at Kirkgate (Leeds) took on his account in 1894, the manager wrote: 'Arranged to take all his money, including copper. The latter to be charged 3d in the £'.

If Michael Marks sold a surprisingly wide variety of articles for one penny on his first stalls, so too did M & S in their first penny bazaar, where in 1902 you could obtain, for example, 'a serviceable pepper box, a nutmeg grater, a candlestick, a fish-slice or a cake-tin', or choose from a huge basket a screwdriver or a pair of pliers.

For purposes of comparison, it is interesting to look at other prices of the time. You could post a letter then for a penny; the rate had not changed since 1840. And you cold buy a common oyster at Billingsgate fish market for a penny also. A cigar cost 5d, a silk umbrella cost 2s 6d, and a watch in a silver case 13s; ladies' corsets were 5s a pair.

According to an article in *Home Chat* in 1903, 'Children are liberally catered for at the penny shop. There are toys in sufficient variety to drive every child frantic with joy'. Men, too, could buy cuff links, collar studs and watch chains at the same time as they bought brooches for their wives. 'The jewellery, it is hardly necessary to state', the same *Home Chat* article cautioned, 'is not guaranteed to be of any particular quality of hall-mark'.

Something of the flavour of the business later in the decade is caught in the pages of the amply illustrated Marks and Spencer *Grand Annual* (complete with

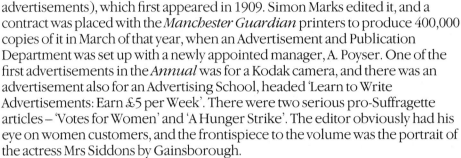

The *Grand Annual*, a mixture of stories, articles, jokes, and advertisements, appeared in four volumes over the period 1909-14. The first volume was edited by Simon Marks. This is the cover of the second volume, 1910-11.

advertisements), which first appeared in 1909. Simon Marks edited it, and a contract was placed with the *Manchester Guardian* printers to produce 400,000 copies of it in March of that year, when an Advertisement and Publication Department was set up with a newly appointed manager, A. Poyser. One of the first advertisements in the *Annual* was for a Kodak camera, and there was an advertisement also for an Advertising School, headed 'Learn to Write Advertisements: Earn £5 per Week'. There were two serious pro-Suffragette articles – 'Votes for Women' and 'A Hunger Strike'. The editor obviously had his eye on women customers, and the frontispiece to the volume was the portrait of the actress Mrs Siddons by Gainsborough.

The *Annual* had a somewhat chequered history and almost disappeared in 1911. It survived in 1912, however, when a new department manager, G. Protheroe, was appointed, and in 1913 and 1914. (Protheroe was in charge of all M & S publications, among them *Our Bairns' First Reading Book* and editions of *Robinson Crusoe* and *The Arabian Nights* in a Mammoth Library series.) Volume II of the *Annual* had a picture of an aeroplane on its cover – it was flying over St Paul's – and Volume IV included a military column, 'Tommy Atkins Here and There'.

In general, the advertisements are more memorable than the short stories and jokes which comprise the main contents, though the titles of the stories (and their illustrations) can be evocative – 'Vengeance is Mine', 'The Curse of Aahnes', 'Children of the Philistines' – and some of the authors were well-known popular writers like W. Pett Ridge and William le Queux. There was not too much exaggeration, therefore, behind the motto of Volume V – 'Everybody's reading it'.

The advertisements then included 'the finest candles', patent medicines, Maypole soap, dyes for home dyeing, best India tape, Phyllis Dare hair-pins, Sphere suspenders, rubber heels, Royal Doncaster butterscotch, Birds' custard, Mendine liquid cement, and Midland furniture (on hire purchase).

There was a Christmas flavour, too, to some of the volumes of the *Annual*, which advertised a '5/- Hamper of Toys' obtainable from M & S by post. It contained 60 articles, including dolls, soldiers, mouth organs, motor cars, boats, mirror puzzles, watches, brooches, dominoes, snakes-and-ladders, ludo and draughts – 'just the thing for parties, Christmas trees, school treats, bazaars, etc.'. There was also a 'Great Xmas Tree Decorators' Parcel', costing five shillings: 'half the charm and mystery of the Magic Tree (in ever-increasing use) is given by the beautiful colour and sheen of the Tinsel Gardens, Jewels and Ornaments with which the boughs are laden'.

This was not the only reference to magic in the *Annual*. Given the bleakness of much of the daily life of many of the M & S customers, retailing as a whole had an air of magic about it in Edwardian times. There was an enormous contrast between the brightly lit store and the dingy rooms in many homes. The maximum working-class purchase in any shop was seldom more than a few shillings. Furniture was the most expensive item bought: a 'plain servant's bed' with woollen mattress cost £1 15s, and a chest of drawers 17s. It was not until the 1920s that the idea of widely distributed mass 'durable consumer goods' began to take shape. When people bought their first wireless sets, some of which cost between £4 and £10, they were said to be buying the most expensive articles they had ever owned.

The principle of a uniform penny price had broken down completely in M&S during the last phases of the First World War, when stocks fell and prices rose. A number of letters written by suppliers after a disastrous fire in 1918 at M&S's Mile End (London) warehouse, when everything was gutted before the firemen arrived, have survived. They give unusual glimpses both of what was obtainable on sales counters during that year and of unprecedented increases in prices. There was a 50% rise, for example, in the prices of hats, postal wrappers, solid blue crayons, hat pins, long crinkle paper, steel and plated thimbles, pairs of black elastic garters and small firescreens. Christmas Candles (in August) went up from 1d to 2d, handkerchiefs and shaving soap from 1½d to 2d, white cups from 2½d to 3d, small teapots from 4d to 6½d, kettles and saucepans from 6d to 7d, and writing pads from 6½d to 9d. A few months later, in October, boracic ointment, cold cream and coconut oil all went up in price from 1d to 1½d, as did feather dusters ('all kinds') and 'dream books'.

The store at Acton, west London, in 1912: note the variety of goods and the use of the pavement for display. This store closed in 1926.

Not surprisingly there was no clear-cut selling policy in M&S during the early 1920s. A *Sale News* sheet produced by the Edgware Road (London) branch about this time concentrates on 'household bargains', ranging from an engraved tumbler at 3d (2s 9d per dozen) to a set of five 'best enamel stew jars at 6s 6d'. In a 'Kiddies' Corner' column clockwork trains with eight rails cost 5s and clockwork motor-bikes 3s 6d. A 'large assortment of stationery' was offered, and 'suitcases of strong fibre' cost 6s, 7s and 8s depending on size. 'We are able to offer these remarkable bargains', the advertisement goes on, 'because we are able to buy in enormous quantities'. And it introduces a selling gimmick unusual in the history of M&S: 'a coupon enabling a shopper at the store to save one penny in the shilling during the coming sale'. There is also reference to a 'new easy-payment system' whereby goods over 4s in value could be laid aside and credit arranged.

Detailed selling lists have survived for the year 1924. Among the earthenware items, narrow fluted plates were selling at 4d and white fluted vegetable dishes at 2s. Jugs ranged in price from 6d to 1s 6d and pudding bowls from 3d to 7½d. Among the enamelware, frying pans cost as little as 6d and shallow milk pans 1s. Kettles were 1s 6d or 2s and teapots 2s 6d. There was a special category of 'yellow ware'. There was also by then a substantial confectionery business: £69 of Regal toffee was sold in Weymouth in one week, more than half on Saturday afternoon. Southend disposed of £126 14s 3d of Southend rock, 10% of its total sales.

The two main departments of M&S from the 1930s onwards – textiles and foods – figure to only a minor extent, if at all, on such inventories or – when the public company was set up in 1926 – in the lists of store departments: 'Haberdashery, Hosiery and Drapery, Toilet Requisites, Glass, China and Earthenware, Stationery, Confectionery, Toys and Sports Goods, Fancy Goods, Jewellery, Gramophones, Records and Music, Cutlery, Household Goods, Hardware, Tin and Enamelware, Books and Novels'. What had happened by then, however, was the formulation of the new 5s price policy, formally introduced in 1927. A year earlier, it had been stated that the prices of all the goods in the stores were below 5s, 'the majority of the goods offered ranging between 1d and 1s'.

By setting a higher limit M&S was forcing itself into a new buying policy. It had to find suppliers able and willing to provide it with a wide range of goods up to 5s. There was another consequence: many traditional categories of goods vanished from the stores to allow the new ones to come in. Indeed, by 1932 over 70% of

51

Right: Window displays in the 1920s: above, Oldham Street, Manchester, at Christmas; below, Eastbourne.

the items listed in the 1926 prospectus had disappeared from the counters of M & S. Some, like china, stationery, haberdashery, earthenware and records, were to return later. But by then social and economic conditions had changed.

In a new *Marks and Spencer Magazine*, which appeared in the summer of 1932 and was introduced by an article 'A Day in the Life of a Queen', there was a clear statement of the 'Nothing sold over 5s' policy. 'M & S amazing values', we read, 'are the result of trading direct with manufacturers for cash. All benefits of price reductions are passed on to our customers'. The influence of 'big orders' and 'M & S enormous buying power' on manufacturers was also stressed. Finally, however, there was a reference to quality. 'M & S do not buy seconds or sub-standard articles. Satisfaction is guaranteed either by a refund of money or exchange of articles'.

There were then over 20 M & S departments 'satisfying the everyday needs of men, women and children' – ladies' and children's drapery; men's and boys' wear; fancy goods; footwear; household linens; gramophone records; confectionery; toiletries; lighting; toys; haberdashery; millinery; china; enamel and aluminium ware; stationery; and special toys and gifts. Children's books were also among the lines advertised – such as *Romp Time Stories* and *Rascals' Book*.

A new food department had opened in 1931 selling fruit, vegetables and canned goods. And in 1933, when one of the slogans of the day was 'Eat more fruit', a separate fruit department was in being (dealing in Jaffa oranges and grapefruit from Palestine and apples and tomatoes from Britain), to be followed four years later by the establishment of a fruit-distribution centre in Covent Garden.

The deliberate reduction of unplanned old lines and the introduction of planned new lines simplified M & S business. The rate of turnover, which had worried William Chapman, increased while profit margins on single items tended to fall. There was no need for large-scale special annual sales of the kind that before 1914 had had more of the theatre than of the store about them. Marks and Sieff were more like scientists than impresarios in what they bought and sold, testing demand through sample ranges in a limited number of stores and adjusting prices when they thought it necessary.

There was a continuing demand throughout the 1930s for household goods, as more new houses were built, many of them on council estates. But M & S specialised in items like the opening special at the new Marble Arch store in 1930 – a tin kettle, price 6d, in two styles. In the same year, a 'watch week' was held in all major M & S stores, during which 'unbreakable watches' were on sale at 2s 11d and 3s 11d each. Watches remained a favourite M & S purchase during the 1930s.

The main thrust of expansion during the years between 1932 and 1939 was in textiles, whose sales multiplied threefold, so that in 1939 they represented two-thirds of the company's total sales. Women, men and children were all catered for systematically, with emphasis from the start on design, quality, value and display. As Simon Marks put it in his address to M & S shareholders in 1934, 'It is the function of the modern distributor to help consumers to purchase ... healthier and more attractive clothing .... We have to strike a right balance between variety and uniformity, for if uniformity makes for economy in production, it is variety which makes the appeal to the purchaser. We aim at

Window displays in the 1930s. From the top: men's ties and ladies' overalls in trial displays at Michael House, Baker Street; oranges at Brighton.

standardisation of basic fabrics, but we avoid standardised uniformity in the finished article.... The period is long past when low prices meant low quality and bad taste'.

There were still marked social differences in clothes, however. Working-men's best Sunday suits (and haircuts) were as unmistakable as Savile Row suits, and the most fashionable women's outfits of the 1920s and 1930s could not have been worn by working-class women even if they had been able to afford them.

By the time the Pantheon opened in 1938, footwear was a prominent M & S item, with separate display fixtures for 'men's, youths' and boys' shoes, and for ladies' fashion shoes, comfort (or matrons') shoes, slippers, and children's and infants' shoes'. There was also 'one of the biggest dress sections ever provided by a variety store'. 'Rows upon rows of garment rails', it was proudly announced (they were a new feature) 'show a "forest" of wearing apparel for infants, boys and girls, and women...'.

The range of clothing on offer at all M & S stores was wide: from hosiery to blouses, tailored shirts, night-dresses and pyjamas. Men's woven-poplin shirts in the 1930s cost 5s, winceyette pyjamas 3s 11d (in the cold houses of the period winceyette was a popular material), ladies' spun-rayon dresses 5s (rayon became the first named synthetic fibre in 1924), and children's frocks 1s 11d.

The blouse, which might cost as little as 2s 11d, was something of an M & S speciality, and it is interesting to compare M & S blouses of the 1930s with blouses of the Edwardian period, with their high boned collars and delicately worked fronts. The M & S blouse was simple, neat and easy to wash. Hooks and eyes were a thing of the past. So, too, in time was the steel-boned corset, the decline of which was even more significant in retrospect than the decline of the crinoline in the nineteenth century.

There was a connection, of course, between changes in eating habits (and nutritional standards) and dress. The slim shape became the fashion during the 1920s, but several generations would pass before it became an objective of older women as well as of 'flappers'. The kind of foods M & S sold during the 1920s and 1930s, beginning with sweets and chocolate in 1924, were certainly not slimming-type foods. By 1939, however, sales of food already accounted for one fifth of the company's turnover, as compared with just over a tenth in 1932. In 1930 biscuits (sold by weight) first appeared on the counters, as did slab cake and swiss rolls in 1933, to be followed in 1934 and 1935 by sausages, cooked meats, pies, cheese and bacon.

There were also developments in catering. Ice cream had been sold since 1927 – at first in solid blocks which had to be cut into briquettes – and in 1935 and 1936 cafés were opened in Leeds, Bradford and London (Marble Arch), where customers could order from 'popular' menus joints, chops, steaks or the inevitable fish and chips. By 1938 there were 21 catering installations, 8 of them tea-bars only and 5 of them fish-bars.

This was a new line of business for M & S, and many of the existing stores were not equipped to handle it. More space was demanded than was often available, and it took time to establish links between kitchen and laboratory. Mistakes were made, particularly before a departmental head was specially appointed in 1938 to apply M & S experience in other merchandising to catering. Thereafter full menus were eliminated, and the range of dishes was simplified and their quality improved. The timing from a business point of view was good, because once war broke out in 1939 there was an increased demand for eating outside the home. Indeed, by March 1941 M & S had 32 catering centres and a year later 82. The turnover in March 1942 was four times as great as in the previous year.

Catering might be a war-time financial success, but during the war sales both of textiles and of food were subject to tight restrictive control. The first effect of the war was to clear stocks of canned and bottled foods and tins of biscuits from the counters almost at once. Stocking of food, indeed, passed from the store to the home. A longer-term effect was the development of rationing through the ingenious 'points' system. As the sale of textiles became more complicated, clothes rationing, which started in 1941 and which was organised on a coupon basis, with different numbers of coupons buying different types of clothing, did not harm M & S as much as most of its competitors. Indeed, the company benefited from the Utility Scheme, because Utility clothes, which closely followed M & S standard specifications, contributed the bulk of the company's turnover in clothing and were exempt from purchase tax.

It is significant that in clothing collections in national and regional museums, which concentrate mainly on 'middle-class' clothes, it is only from the late 1940s and 1950s onwards that M & S items begin to appear and many of them are St Michael Utility garments – such as a blue and white striped cotton blouse, *c.* 1943-5, at Worthing and a salmon-coloured cotton bra at Oldham. The Blaise Castle House Museum at Bristol, which possesses a valuable collection of nineteenth- and twentieth-century clothing (with an invaluable Utility collection and a 'haberdasher's shop' complete with original packaging, labels and price tags) has eight M & S items, including a 1940s dress (St Michael with Utility label) in blue fabric printed with a striking, multi-coloured pattern of grape-vines and exotic birds.

Above: Aluminium ware at Blackpool in 1932.

The Utility Scheme remained in operation until 1952 (and in modified form until 1955), but during these years of austerity more interesting things were happening behind the scenes than on the counters, particularly in relation to new synthetic fibres. Nylon had become available in Britain for the first time in 1941 but it was not until after the war, when there was no longer a demand for parachutes, that M & S in 1947 was able to offer its first nylon fabric blouse to the public. Terylene, too, was a war-time baby, developed by the Calico Printers' Association in 1941 and kept a secret until 1945. In 1947 ICI acquired world rights in it (except for the United States), and full-scale production began in 1955 with the introduction of blends of terylene and wool. M & S was enthusiastic about it, describing it in 1954 as 'the wonder fabric of the future'.

Other articles on sale at the end of 1954 were Jaffa oranges, Brazil nuts (unobtainable during the war), cakes for home icing (a new line), 'provocatively sheer 15 denier nightdresses', fisherman's knit jumpers, and a wide range of slippers (sales of which were said to be double that at Christmas 1953). There was another new synthetic material here – vinyl. And the message for 1955 in *St Michael News* was that this was 'the time to promote': 'A good sales promotion is like a searchlight. Before its beams the merchandise is revealed in all its potential'.

A *Display Manual* had been prepared seven years earlier, which began with the

More examples of window displays from the 1930s, giving an idea of the enormous range of goods on sale. The cans of milk and cream (opposite page, in colour) date from the 1950s.

words 'Few things have changed more during our life-time than the practice of display'. It stressed 'eye appeal' and the need for showcards 'which often tell a sales story'. And it reinforced a favourite M & S principle – 'Display is more forceful than newspaper advertising, because the public see the actual article displayed'.

Like everything else in retailing, the techniques of display were to change drastically during the unprecedented expansion of M & S business which began during the late 1950s, when there were striking changes in the appearance and layout of the stores and in their use of selling space. 'The present-day growing range of quality goods could not be successfully displayed in the smaller sales areas, with dark wooden floors, heavy mahogany-coloured counters and surrounding panelling, tungsten lighting, etc. of the "chain store" of earlier years', Wilfred Norris wrote in a report of 1961 on 'The Development of the Size and Character of our Stores', and twenty-two years later, as design interests have changed, the emphasis now is on 'the warmer and more colourful look', 'more inviting' and 'more attractive to younger customers'. 'The total environment' or 'ambience' of the store is being worked on, and all store features, including signs and promotional material, related to it. Experiments were taking place in 1983 in Coventry and Uxbridge, and the new stores at Epsom and Brentwood implement the new approach.

An article by David Churchill in the *Financial Times* in March 1983 described vividly the difference between the range of goods which were by then available in M & S stores as compared with the early years of market stalls and penny bazaars. It was headed 'M & S products change its image'. About half M & S annual sales, he pointed out, were of products which had been sold for the first time within the previous five years – though he did not mention that some of them, like gifts, books and toiletries, had returned in a new guise after a long absence.

Once again M & S was both responding to social change and accelerating it through a wider range, in particular, for the kitchen and the bathroom. Clocks, like watches, had been a favourite M & S product during the 1920s. Now a new brass kitchen clock was introduced. Utensils had been one of the earliest products sold, as had tablecloths. But now the utensils included chopping boards and casserole stands. Bedding was now sold with matching wallpaper, curtains and ceramics.

In the case of toiletries, reintroduced in the mid-1970s, M & S have, as always, learnt through experience. It was found that 15% of the products accounted for 80% of the sales, and as a result the range was reduced. Soaps and cosmetics had figured, of course, in a very different range (and quality) of products even in the earliest days of Michael Marks and Tom Spencer. Now, simply, practically and attractively packed and displayed by product group (with descriptions attached), they were offered as 'distinctively high quality merchandise at competitive prices'.

In textiles there has been an increasing emphasis on fashion – including colour (and colour coordination) as well as style – and on whole ensembles as well as individual items of clothing. It began with women's clothes and spread to clothes for children and men. In seven years from 1976 the M & S share of the market for women's dresses increased from about 7% to about 12% of the United Kingdom home market.

A typical modern store: Enfield, opened in November 1982.

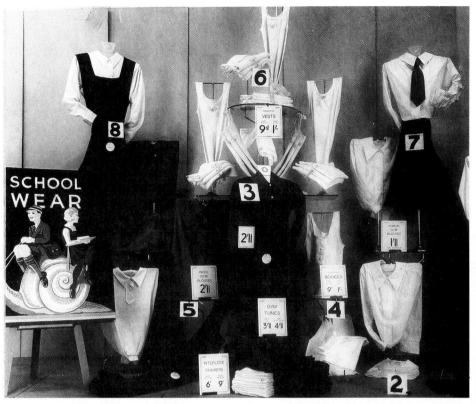

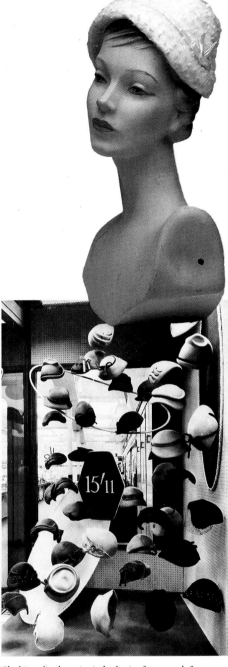

Clothing displays. Anti-clockwise from top left:
schoolwear, 1937; stockings and dresses, mid-1930s;
millinery, 1955.

No intensive attempt had been made during the 1960s and 1970s to tap the growing teenager and young-adult market (and just beyond), and although in September 1979 a brand-new department of young fashions was put on sale in a range called 'Miss Michelle', it was no more successful than a 'Young St Michael' range had been in 1970. M & S was not competing with the smaller and more specialised boutiques, although it was aware of their influence on tastes. Yet younger children were particularly well catered for in the 1960s, and M & S children's clothes are represented in several galleries. At the Camberley Museum a girl's skirt and school blouse and 'one pair of dark grey boys' shorts elasticated at the back of the waistband' are on display, while at the Buckinghamshire County Museum there is a polyester T-shirt printed with *The Muppet Show* and seven pictures of the Muppets (*c.* 1977).

At the Churchill Gardens Museums, Hereford, there are men's pyjamas (*c.* 1969) and at Leicester trousers (*c.* 1971, aubergine polyester/wool, flared bottoms), which reveal how increasingly fashion-conscious M & S men's clothing designs became during the 1960s and 1970s. Men's suits were introduced in 1972, the first bulk quantities of them produced by foreign manufacturers. Ten years later, when the business had expanded to 200 stores, 55% of them were British-made (the rest came from Italy, Finland and Israel). In the first six months of 1983, sales were up on the same period of 1982 by 30%, at a time when the British suit market as a whole had declined from sales of 10 million suits in 1972 to less than 5 million in 1982.

The return to wool in one distinctive range of suits in the 1980s is interesting in relation to changing tastes. 'We are now appealing to a different customer', the Men's Suit Department stated in 1983. 'For example, we have discovered after several tries that we can now sell wool suits all the year round by varying the fabric weight according to season'. Cotton, too, had been re-discovered – 'so cool, so crisp, and so comfortable' – and from 1977 onwards it figured more prominently in M & S clothes, including shirts, an M & S speciality.

It is in relation to food sales, perhaps, that the biggest of all the M & S merchandising revolutions has taken place. The cafés and café-bars of the war soon went; Leeds and Exeter, the last two survivors, were closed in 1961. The sale of ice cream, which was too untidy a product to eat in the new M & S stores, went too. In their place came many completely new products, from avocados to fresh poultry. And old products enjoyed a new life. Biscuits boomed. Cakes sales increased by 5½ times between 1965 and 1967. Sandwiches were reintroduced in five stores in 1980, the first of them salmon and tomato; the fastest selling line, prawn and mayonnaise, was introduced in 1981.

Indian and Chinese foods were first tried in 1974. The products were frozen and mainly boil-in-bag. They included chow mein and tandoori chicken. The time was not yet ripe, however, for their general distribution and although tandoori chicken returned in 1977, it was not until 1982 that a different range was launched, including crispy pancakes and pork spare ribs. They were soon available in 200 stores, and further Indian foods were introduced on trial in February 1983 with 'initial reaction' reported as 'very good'. They included chicken korma, tikka kebabs and pilau rice. This time M & S concentrated on freshly prepared products which were sold from cold chain counters rather than from frozen food tubs.

The Times published an article by Nicholas Wapshott in March 1983 on M & S foods under the title 'Haute Cuisine from a Wire Basket'. 'Who outside the ranks of the well-to-do had ten years ago indulged in the delights of red and green capsicums (the posh names for peppers)', the author asked; 'the delicate delights of the mange-tout (pealets still in their shells); the wonder of courgettes (neo-marrows); the crisp chomp of fennel; or sucked the slender fingers of asparagus? All are our staple M & S fare'. And in August 1983 M & S swept the board in the first Fast Foodfax poll from Cambridge Market Research by winning 11 out of the top 20 places. Today foods account for more than one third of M & S sales in the United Kingdom. The company sells a million chickens every week and has become Britain's largest fishmonger.

What to sell remains an unending quest. Wine was first sold in 1973. The initial range was eight wines, four sherries and a small range of beers. There are now nearly 50 wines, and sales rose from £0.1 million in 1973 to £35 million in 1983.

To understand how the quest for new products continues, it is necessary to trace how M & S decides what to buy and where to buy it. M & S has learnt how to test as well as how to select so as to ensure quality and value. Before it goes on sale every St Michael product, and where necessary its individual components, is comprehensively tested in both the laboratory and in use. For example, every Friday afternoon at about 4.30 a messenger tours the sixth and seventh floors of Michael House, M & S headquarters in Baker Street, delivering a plain, white plastic bag to a number of selected M & S employees so that they can taste for themselves new food items on offer. Everything sold is carefully tested in M & S kitchens. Those involved in creating the product regularly visit stores to learn more about the market at first hand, and all directors and senior Head Office personnel visit stores frequently and informally. They are following a pattern established by Simon Marks, and they have encouraged their manufacturers to follow in their footsteps also. There are 790 suppliers, and many of them have come to learn as much about customers as M & S has learnt about technology.

Above: M & S has become one of Britain's major wine retailers.

Below, left: An ice-cream sundae counter at Holloway, London, in the 1930s. Sales of ice-cream to eat on the premises ceased in 1961.

STOCKROOM AT A NEW STORE AND (INSET)
A COUNTER BASKET AND GOODS FROM A PRE-1914 BAZAAR

WHERE TO BUY

'Silly people say there is no friendship in business', we read in an article of 1932 in the *M & S Magazine*. 'The truth is there is no business without friendship. In other words, we cannot help ourselves without helping you. Nobody can. That is a rule of life'.

The article was written mainly for M & S customers, who were told that M & S had carefully devised 'an elaborate system' with the intention of 'making every one of its customers richer'. Yet the main point of the article, which was called 'The Buyer and the Seller Gossip Together', was to emphasise the importance of the relationship between M & S and the companies from which it bought the goods selling in its stores. 'We add to your wages', it told customers, 'by introducing the girl who makes the stockings to the girl who wears them'.

This is a neat and simple statement concerning a system which was to become far more sophisticated after 1932. M & S was never to manufacture any of the goods it sold, but it was to inspect its suppliers' plants as well as to test their products and to employ its own technologists to ensure high quality and to promote product innovation. What is sold in the stores today is the result of a continuous collaboration with suppliers. There is strict quality control. There is also a highly sophisticated delivery system, built up between 1971 and 1981, with regional depots that coordinate all deliveries. The use of larger, standard-sized lorries has reduced the number of deliveries needed to accommodate stores.

From its beginning M & S developed direct and friendly relationships with particular manufacturers. Thus, William Chapman himself, who sold handkerchiefs to M & S, was Tom Spencer's friend; and Michael Marks in the week before he died had been visiting chocolate manufacturers in Scotland and makers of cans of tinned milk (at a penny a can) in Eire. During the early years before 1914 the advantages of bulk buying were already fully appreciated, and large orders were confirmed at board meetings. In February 1908, for example, an order for 3,500 gross of buttons was placed with Buttons Limited, and another order of 1,860 gross of an unspecified product was placed with a firm called Chamberlain and Hill.

A number of letters to and from suppliers survives from 1918. Even at that time M & S suppliers were scattered throughout the country, most of them specialists in particular lines, like C.H. Parsons & Brother, soap manufacturers, of Manchester; Eli Heyworth and Sons of Manchester, 'makers of extra quality long cloths and cambrics, lawns, voiles, twills, sateens, etc'; The Nugget Polish Company of Kennington Oval; and Petty and Sons, 'wholesale and export commercial and colour printers and lithographers' of Leeds. There were a few big suppliers, too, notably Lever Brothers of Port Sunlight.

All the letters point to price increases. 'Today's prices are 75% to 80% over March prices', said J.T. Darlington of Aston (Birmingham), a timber merchant, 'manufacturer of flag stickers and poles' and 'wholesale dealer in flags'. 'You secured exceptional advantages in placing your orders so far in advance', Petty and Sons noted, 'large quantities of the books recently delivered are printed on paper bought over 3 years ago'. But now supplies were short, and labour costs rising: 'only last week we were presented with a memorial [petition] for a further 10s per week'. The Star Brush Company of Holloway (London) feared that while it would soon be able to supply 'brushes similar to those supplied before the war, prices will be a long time coming down to the pre-war levels, if they ever do'.

It took time for M & S after 1918 to build up the kind of relationships with manufacturers which were to establish its distinctive reputation. One of M & S's most happy and creative relationships has been with Corah's of Leicester. But this seemed unlikely in 1926 when Israel Sieff first approached this old family firm. Corah's had been manufacturing 'St Margaret's' hosiery and underwear since 1866 and other textile articles, including mittens, gaiters and bathing wear, since 1873; and, not surprisingly, the Corah family feared in 1926 that if they were to supply these lines in bulk directly to M & S, they would lose their traditional trade with other smaller clients. They would also face the hostility of the Wholesale Textile Association. Sieff's first approaches were rebuffed, therefore – he was treated like an interloper – and it was only with difficulty that Cecil Coleman, the General Manager of the business, who might have lost his job for talking to Sieff, persuaded J.R. and J.H. Corah to respond to the M & S offer.

The trade started with a parcel of children's socks, and business deals amounting to £859 had been arranged by the end of the year. According to Keith Jopp, the historian of Corah's, the relationship was pursued with great vigour and determination by both sides during the years that followed. In years of depression Corah's, like M & S, actually expanded; in years of war M & S moved part of their office to Leicester and an even greater sense of friendly 'inter-dependability' was achieved; and in the post-austerity years of M & S expansion a new phase of quality development began with M & S as Corah's largest customer demanding 'better and more stylish garments' than ever before.

By 1966, when new Corah's factories had been opened and annual trade ran into millions of pounds, Robert Wessel, then chairman of Corah's, praised Coleman, Marks and Sieff as 'men of vision and courage' who had prepared the way for a very special relationship, and he was willing to proclaim proudly that Corah's

Above: A corner of the display-material section in a modern store stockroom.

Below: Letterheads of a selection of typical M & S suppliers in the first two decades of the century.

believed in the 'same philosophy' as M & S and had the 'same sense of purpose…Lord Marks in his lifetime inspired us to reach out beyond the bounds of our capacity. He generated a sense of purpose and service among all of us'.

Already by the late 1920s and early 1930s M & S had worked out a distinctive buying policy of its own, directly affecting its suppliers, which set out to avoid what Simon Marks called 'guess work' and 'hit and miss' methods and which laid emphasis on quality as well as on price. It was clearly expressed by Israel Sieff, whom Simon Marks had called in to develop it, at the Annual General Meeting of 1931, when he explained how M & S was 'paying increasing attention to the quality and finish of our goods'. 'If necessary', he went on, 'we help our manufacturer to select, and to purchase under the most favourable conditions, his raw materials. We see no reason why an article, because it is low priced, should not have most of the refinements and neatness of the higher-priced article'.

When an early bulk order for M & S enabled Corah's to offer women's stockings at 8s 6d – 1s a dozen cheaper than would have had to be paid to a wholesaler – there were discussions between M & S and Corah's as to how best to use this differential to improve the quality of the product. There and elsewhere M & S was deliberately 'encouraging its manufacturers to become more efficient' and also 'educating' them.

Innovation and care were felt to go together. And so it was, too, in the dealings between M & S and Dewhirst's, the oldest of all M & S's business contacts. Dewhirst's supplied goods, mainly working clothes, to M & S during the 1930s, but it was during the 1950s, 1960s and 1970s that the scale of operations was dramatically extended in collaboration with M & S. In 1955, on the death of his father, Alistair J. ('Sandy') Dewhirst became Chairman and Joint Managing Director of the I.J. Dewhirst group of companies, which were mainly involved in wholesaling. Sales at that time were £686,016 – they included a limited manufacturing output (men's and boys' shirts, in particular) for M & S – and profits stood at £19,195. By 1982 sales were £23 million, 90% of which was to M & S, and profits over £2½ million. A key event in the history of the business had been the decision, taken in 1950, to manufacture textiles outside Leeds – at Driffield in the East Riding of Yorkshire, where Dewhirst's gave employment to a large number of women workers who had hitherto been offered few alternative forms of employment to domestic service. In the words of one of their shareholders, a local chemist who retired from business in 1982 after forty years, the Dewhirsts not only brought prosperity to the market town but ushered in a 'social revolution' of which the suffragette leader Mrs Pankhurst would have been proud. That was not the only social revolution. 'Leisurewear' was beginning to be in greater demand than 'workwear'; indeed the hitherto sharp distinction between the two was narrowing. Like M & S Dewhirst's were to benefit from social change, and in 1976 we read that 'the Company had moved successfully into the area of leisurewear, which is a "growth market"'.

After I.J. Dewhirst Holdings Ltd became a public company in October 1972 – with the invaluable support of M & S – another purpose-built factory was erected at Pennywell (Sunderland), where men's suits would be produced to M & S specifications. It began production with a heavy investment in advanced automatic machinery in December 1973. Already at the first meeting of the

M & S has enjoyed particularly long and close links with its clothing suppliers. Two of the most important are Dewhirst's, with whom links go back 100 years, and Corah's of Leicester, who have made M & S clothing since 1926.

Below, left: Menswear at Dewhirst's Peterlee factory. Top and bottom, right: Inside Corah factories in the 1930s and 1980s. Bottom, left: Trial display at Michael House, Baker Street, in the 1930s.

shareholders at York earlier in the year it was announced that profits had exceeded the forecast by 10%. J. M. H. Samuel, the M & S director who proposed the vote of thanks, could declare handsomely: '… as to the conduct of the business, and I can comment with the advantage of some inside knowledge, it has been no less than one would expect of true Yorkshiremen. They have remained in the forefront in the maintenance of the highest quality standards and in the innovation of new and successful ranges of merchandise. These are the two factors which make up the lifeblood of our industry'.

In six years the company's turnover with M & S rose from £1 million to £5 million. Meanwhile, Marcus Sieff was emphasising how close he felt the relationship with British industry had become. The idea of selling stylish suits at reasonable prices, he noted, had been influenced by what was happening overseas, but the switch to British production, he told his shareholders, was a good example of what Britain could do. 'We found suppliers with modern production methods abroad producing suits of better quality, value and design than those produced here. With knowledge gained abroad and the help of Swedish consultants, two major manufacturers at home have developed factories especially engineered, which now supply a substantial proportion of our suits'. The Dewhirst factory at Pennywell was one of them.

Norman Sussman, a main supplier of shirts to M & S, wrote in 1983: 'Without M & S support, without their encouragement and involvement in the development of their suppliers, there would not be any shirt manufacture of significance in the United Kingdom at the present time, for the sales of St Michael shirts account for 50% of UK production, providing a manufacturing base without which the whole viability of the shirt industry could well be questioned'.

It is clear that the policies on buying and dealing with suppliers, enunciated by Israel Sieff, still stand firm. They have required knowledge and good will on both sides and the development of new organisations within M & S itself. And in this connection it was textiles which led the way.

First, a merchandising committee was formed in 1933 to coordinate the work of the various buying departments. Second, in order to carry out scientific and technical research on textile products, a small textile laboratory was set up in 1935, in the first instance restricting its role to testing samples of merchandise from different manufacturers in an attempt to identify faults and to achieve consistency of quality. Third, a Merchandise Development Department was created in 1936 – along with a Design Department – with a mandate to improve the quality and appearance of M & S goods on sale. It included both executives and technical staff and was headed by a chemist, a refugee from Nazi Germany, Dr Eric Kann, who had been employed in Germany by the chain-store firm of Samuel Schocken. Kann's specialised knowledge and experience were exactly what Marks and Sieff needed. The art of buying was being supplemented by the science of product analysis.

This new system was to develop dramatically during the late 1950s, particularly after the concentration of all the head office staff in the new Michael House in Baker Street, where there was substantial laboratory space. Yet even earlier than that, a new Textile Testing Laboratory had been opened in 1946, the Design Department had been extended, and in 1947 a Factory Organisation section, later to be called the Production Engineering Department, had been set up: it was designed 'to assist manufacturers in the progressive modernisation of their plant,

and to adapt themselves to the latest technical advances'. In 1962 minimum standards and test methods were rationalised and set out in book form for manufacturers and finishers.

One of the objects was to encourage manufacturers, dyers and finishers to install adequate testing equipment themselves and to advise them on layout, equipment, methods and training of staff. By 1964 there were already 140 suppliers who had done this. Yet, while the consulting service was strengthened, M & S technologists continued with innovations of their own. Thus they helped to develop a machine for attaching straps to lingerie, which resulted in an increase in output of about 40% and the replacement of skilled sewing machinists in this work by semi-skilled loaders.

Production engineering was concerned with food also, and paid increasing attention to such processes as pre-packing vegetables. Most important of all in this connection, a Food Development Department was created in 1948, with the first of its objects 'the merchandising of a limited range of products in the early stages of development to ensure that both the merchandising departments and the food technologists concentrated their efforts on raising and establishing the standards of a number of basic products'. Other objects included 'encouragement of suppliers to cooperate with the Company's technologists on the development of new lines, on methods of production and on quality and hygienic standards', and to engender 'a spirit of refusal to "accept things as they are", of applying scientific enquiry in … daily work, of asking "how and why" and following up the answers as quickly as possible'.

There were the same 'close, personal and friendly relations with suppliers' in the food business as in textiles, as the business was transformed radically through increased mechanisation, use of new materials, refrigeration, improved packing and loading processes, and bulk handling. M & S technologists, headed by N. Goldenberg, played a key role in the transformation, always setting high standards, while recognising, as J. Edward Sieff put it, that not all the wisdom in the country was to be found in Baker Street.

Suppliers were encouraged to send their representatives to Michael House to discuss what was happening. Simple things mattered as much as complicated ones, and great emphasis was placed on freshness and on grading. Testing on arrival of standard products, like oranges, was one of the most necessary elements in the system. Boxes of oranges from Israel were opened and samples were tasted and checked for skin smoothness, thinness and freedom from blemish, and, if for any reason the boxes were 'opening badly' (that is, if there was a high proportion of rejects), on-the-spot conferences were called and, if necessary, consignments rejected. There were also M & S visits to Israel to discuss packing methods.

Perhaps the newest of all the relationships with suppliers is with farms. In order to secure more attractive farm products, M & S pioneered new ventures. One has been called – in a film made for M & S – 'the crisp-heart lettuce story'. In 1975 no crisp-heart lettuces of the American 'Iceberg' variety were sold by M & S. By 1982 M & S sales amounted to £4 million, two-thirds of the total sales of lettuce. In 1975 'curly' or 'floppy' lettuce was being sold: the coarse wrapper leaves were wasted, the size of its heart unpredictable. 'We wanted', the Food Department

Above: Testing a product in the Food Laboratory at Michael House. Laboratory work at headquarters includes not only testing of products and packaging but also research into product improvement and innovation, often in cooperation with suppliers' technologists.

Below: Proofs of a new tin container for St Michael cosmetics.

Above left: The Design Department at Michael House; and below left, textile colour swatches. Top right: Buying Department at Michael House in the 1930s and (below) 1980s clothing samples. Bottom right: An advertisement from *M&S Magazine*, 1932.

Selecting tomatoes for quality and uniformity of size and colour at a supplier's farm.

stated simply, 'to offer our customers a better eating and better value lettuce'.

To this end a food technologist from M & S went to the United States to study growing and post-harvest technology. A number of United Kingdom suppliers were then identified, each with their own mobile field packhouses that enabled them to cut, wrap, select and box lettuces in a single operation, followed by rapid vacuum cooling to take the 'field heat' out of the lettuce. To allow the cooler to work efficiently, a perforated polypropylene film was used for wrapping the lettuce, and this too helped to preserve quality by preventing further dehydration. Through hard work on the part of the suppliers as well as clear thinking on the part of the food technologists, the UK operation proved a success.

The UK crisp-heart season runs, however, only from the beginning of June to the end of October. The next M & S challenge was to supply customers with crisp-heart lettuce all the year round. The company turned to Spain, which has developed into an important source, and to Israel, where there were further challenges to face on the spot. Cooperation with Israeli Ministry of Agriculture technologists was the first step if 'Iceberg' was to be cultivated in the desert. The next was to work out commercial arrangements with Saphir, one of the Hunter Group of Companies, to achieve a well-organised quality-control and transport network, and Agrexco, Israel's agricultural export company, which markets high-quality produce under the Carmel trade-name. The location chosen was the Moshav Zofar, a small settlement of 27 families in the region of Arava, near the Dead Sea, and the initial investment of capital was £40,000. The project started in November 1981.

A final factor of crucial importance was to move the lettuce from Moshav Zofar to M & S stores in the United Kingdom within 48 hours. To do this a mobile packhouse was introduced. From picking to packing took less than 5 minutes; within 1 hour the lettuces had reached a centre 3 miles north of the settlement, where they were vacuum cooled; 9 hours after picking, they were at Ben Gurion International Airport (Tel Aviv) in a special M & S area; with 11 hours still to go they were safely through the Heathrow customs; and 2 hours after that they were at the Saphir Eurocentre at Faversham (Kent), where they were checked and finally given the M & S seal of approval. In the film they arrive on the fresh foods counter of an M & S store 45 minutes early.

If long journeys are a part of the relationships between the company and its suppliers, M & S has always tried to buy British wherever it can. It has worked well with large and well-known firms such as Courtauld, with whom M & S business totals £150 million a year, and also with firms with an exciting pioneering history, like the Nottingham Manufacturing Company, built up by the Djanogly family who first came to Britain from Germany in the late 1930s; M & S business with them now exceeds £100 million a year. As early as 1927, at M & S's first Annual General Meeting, Simon Marks told the shareholders that M & S purchased 'in this country practically 90% of our requirements', and exactly the same theme was being iterated 54 years later, when Lord Sieff told the shareholders that 'more than 90% of our clothing, household textiles and footwear were manufactured in the United Kingdom', and that three out of four St Michael garments were made from fabric produced in this country. Such quotations demonstrate a remarkable continuity of commitment in changing circumstances. And the whole of the staff was committed to the same objective.

There are two key groups of M & S staff concerned with the buying process: selectors, so described since the 1930s, and merchandisers. Selectors were rightly picked out in 1955 as being 'very special to M & S...constantly on the go, always alert'. It was and is their task to select the goods which are sold in the stores, and they have to be knowledgeable not only about current and probable future tastes and fashions, but about manufacturing methods and the particular capabilities of each supplier. They work closely, of course, with the M & S technologists, who recognise (as Dr Eric Kann put it in his address to the Second World Congress on Man-Made Fibres in 1962) that the retailer is an essential element in the development process, not just the institution at the last sales point.

The merchandisers, working in close cooperation with the selectors, translate the business of the Buying Department into sales. It is their task to watch store demand and turnover, to determine the right size of the order to place with the manufacturers, to ensure that production targets are reached at the right time, to check that production is adjusted in the light of sales, and to ensure smooth distribution to the stores.

The separation of function between selectors and merchandisers has been built into the M & S system, with both groups, like the technologists, as much concerned with innovation (and with fashion) as with habit. Together they have ensured that M & S was in the forefront of the synthetic-fibres revolution and of the fast-foods revolution. Together with their suppliers they have not only responded to customers' needs but have anticipated them. There are many examples of successful achievement, some of which may be ahead of the times. In 1982, for example, a new toothpaste was introduced, in a can just like an aerosol. Every drop of toothpaste could be pressed out of the can (though it has yet to supplant the old-fashioned tube). In food Hunter Foods, which opened a new £1 million fresh and chilled foods plant in November 1983, have pioneered completely new M & S lines, like oranges in caramel and Chinese-style stir-fry vegetables.

The role of technical innovation in commercial enterprise varies from product to product, and sometimes the new technology comes from abroad. Even when there has been relatively little technological advance there has been highly effective commercial adaptation. Thus, in the same year Lambert Howarth, Peter Black and Fiona Footwear were producing new footwear lines at lower prices than M & S had been able to get in the United Kingdom two years before. Peter Black of Keighley is a good example of a post-war firm which has developed through the closest association with M & S selectors. Its business is now over £50 million a year, of which about a half goes to M & S, covering a wide range of products, including bags, footwear, cushions, and toiletries. And it all started with shopping bags for M & S, made initially from Army-surplus materials.

A 1930s Beardmore tractor and trailer restored and repainted for the centenary celebrations.

SHOPPERS OUTSIDE OLDHAM STREET, MANCHESTER, STORE IN 1925

SHOPPERS

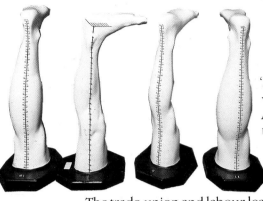

'Satisfaction is a happy customer leaving a store with the goods she wanted', begins an article in *St Michael News* in June 1977. It is almost a business truism and it does not hint at the changes in perception of what customers, male or female, have actually wanted at different periods of M & S history.

The trade-union and labour leader Ernest Bevin, who was Labour Minister in Winston Churchill's war-time coalition government and Foreign Secretary in Clement Attlee's Labour government which succeeded it, used to talk of 'poverty of desire' as the greatest obstacle in the way of working-class emancipation.

Diets in the 1920s varied greatly from one class group to another – and from one region to another – although in the years since then they have come to vary far less. So, too, have clothes. It is taken for granted now that customers have more in common than they have differences.

There are, of course, different physical sizes in different parts of the country. Glasgow and Bournemouth contrast sharply in their ratios of large and small customers, as do Wales and East Anglia, so that M & S has had to map different regional requirements. The human frame varies at least as much as the social structure. As far as food is concerned, however, customers' habits are more or less standard – though Newcastle customers show an exceptional fondness for Madeira cake.

Income is the main determinant of customer choice, with education and experience (including foreign travel) also playing their part. The first M & S customers were people like Bevin, for when Michael Marks opened his first stall (and Bevin was then three years old) there were around 12½ million manual-worker wage-earners in Britain, as against a mere 620,000 people who were well enough off to be assessed for income tax. If Marks had set out purposefully to acquire customers among the income-tax paying groups, he would have provided a different kind of retailing.

There was a high degree of specialisation – in location as well as in lines of business – in late-nineteenth century retailing, with some of the big department stores already concentrating on the comfortably-off middle classes and with others, like David Lewis's in Liverpool and Manchester, calling themselves 'the Friends of the People'. They offered to provide 'everything useful, convenient and comfortable that experience has been able to produce' and employed publicity methods, particularly at times of their annual or six-monthly sales, which had much in common with those of circus showmen. A few British department stores followed the fashions of Paris set by the Bon Marché, which first opened in 1855. By the mid-1880s, it was employing over 3,000 people and had a turnover of 123 million francs; the French novelist Emile Zola thought that it was a place of poetry as well as of business.

Michael Marks knew nothing of such a retailing world, which was even farther removed from Russian Poland than it was from industrial Leeds. The market in Slonim was an agricultural produce market of the kind which had existed for

Shopping contrasts: above, the interior of an M & S store in the 1950s and, below, shoppers at Sheffield market stall before the First World War.

centuries. Yet Marks's first Leeds customers were said to be not as badly off as working-class people in many other towns. Indeed, in the very year when he opened his stall, the Leeds Medical Officer of Health, giving evidence to a royal commission, referred to 'the opulence of the working classes in Leeds'. 'There are a great many trades and we never suffer from a panic', he went on, 'they are well-to-do people, all people earning good wages'. There was none of the 'wretched squalor' in Leeds that he had known in the East End of London.

During the first period of M & S growth, between 1884 and the outbreak of the First World War in 1914, there were many signs of change in society, but there were also many problems. National income rose at the same rate of over 2% a year as it had done during the previous half century; but at no point between 1900 and 1913 did real wages reach the level of the last two years of the nineteenth century, and there was little change in the quantity of goods and services consumed by the 'average Briton'.

When Seebohm Rowntree explored the incidence of primary poverty in York, not far from Leeds, in 1899, he could seriously claim that the 'minimum necessary annual cost of clothing for a woman' was only just over £1 11s, which nonetheless was comfortably more than a woman's average weekly wage. The list of clothes included a pair of boots, no slippers ('wear old boots'!), one ready-made skirt (8s) and blouse (2s), four aprons, two pairs of stockings (at 9d or 1s), underclothing (one of each article, 2s 10d), one pair of stays, 1 hat ('new one would cost 4s 6d but would last several years'), one jacket (1s 6d), and one shawl (1s). 'Buy a skirt at a jumble sale or go without'. Meanwhile, in Old Bond Street in London, where there were 101 establishments concerned with women's fashions, nothing ready-made could be bought.

What to some customers was 'the age of extravagance', therefore, to others was 'the age of penury'. 'There may be said to be in theory two standards of life', wrote a sociologist in 1910, 'the standard of simple necessities, and the standard of refined and educated necessities. The former can be secured for an average family on about 25s a week, the latter on about £600 a year' (that is, about 250s a week).

In Edwardian Britain M & S was not dealing in 'simple necessities' like bread or bacon or sugar, which were the staples of new mass retailers like Lipton's or Home and Colonial, each with chains of multiple shops. The customers were going to the penny bazaars for what Rowntree called 'extras', and these were not easy to pay for unless they were within the M & S range. Of course, it was fun to have a 'look around', too, and it was significant that many of the M & S bazaars bore the words 'Admission Free' over their doors.

In making his careful calculations about poverty, Rowntree set the most stringent standards before concluding that 10% of the population of York could not afford a minimum standard of living 'bare of all creature comforts'. The mother, for example, could 'never buy any pretty clothes for herself or for her children, the character of the family wardrobe, like the character of the family diet, being governed by the regulation, "Nothing must be bought but that which is absolutely necessary for the maintenance of physical health, and what must be bought must be of the plainest and most economical description"'. Not surprisingly, he never mentioned shops in his book.

In his valuable social history of modern retailing, *The Coming of the Mass Market, 1850-1914* (1981), Hamish Fraser says that the typical shop was not the multiple but 'the small corner shop, where the odour of paraffin added a certain something to the appeal of a few ounces of cheese or a child's candy. The typical firm was not the industrial giant supplying a national or international market, but the small enterprise selling still to a largely regional market'. Nonetheless, it was 'clearly recognised that a mass market had arrived and had to be catered for'.

Given this background, the long-term effect of the First World War was to speed up the process by influencing the customer as much as the producer or the retailer. While in the short run it added to the customer's problems, as it went on it 'disclosed', according to the economist J.M. Keynes, 'the possibility of consumption to all'. And people after the war were claiming 'better maintenance' as a right, whereas hitherto they had often seemed to be begging for it as a privilege.

In general the years between the two world wars have as mixed a reputation with historians as they had with contemporaries. They were bedevilled by heavy unemployment, which never fell below 6.8% of the working population and exceeded 20% in 1932, while old basic industries had gone into all too obvious decline. In the bleak years, 1932 and 1933, almost half the workers in the iron and steel industries, a third of those in coal mining and nearly two thirds of those in shipbuilding were unemployed. There were sharp social contrasts between areas with old basic industries of this kind and more fortunate areas where the new industries of the twentieth century, like electricity, light engineering and chemicals, had developed. On the other hand, for those who were lucky enough

Above: Young shoppers pose outside Upper Street, Islington, store during the First World War.

Below, left: Store interior in the 1950s. Below: The café bar at Exeter shortly before its closure in 1961. Bottom: Leeds store in 1951.

to be employed during the 1930s, falling prices meant that life was substantially cheaper than it had been. Average annual income, calculated at constant (1900) prices, rose from £44 per head in 1913 to £57 per head in 1938.

These were the years when M & S began to take on its modern shape within a new national pattern of retailing. Whatever else languished, large-scale retailing flourished. Other large organisations were gaining a bigger share of the retail trade also, so that on the eve of the Second World War in 1939, while single-unit small shops still accounted for 88% of the total number of retail establishments, they were now dealing in only 66% of the total trade. Customers liked the new super-stores and the new kind of shopping, and already customers were beginning to behave more and more like each other, whatever their social background. Nonetheless, Len Cohen, the first manager at Marble Arch, who moved there from managing at Nottingham, found many of his customers there snobbish, 'buying', they said, 'not for themselves but for the maid'. It still was not feasible, as a new generation of social surveyors pointed out, for a working-class family to aspire to anything approaching the standards of the family of the middle-class salary earner, let alone 'the rich'.

The attitudes of customers of the early 1930s at a different level were described in the *M & S Magazine* in the summer of 1932. It included a fascinating article 'How to get Two Pounds' worth for a Pound: Mrs Goodwife goes out Shopping'. Mrs

Her wardrobe			His wardrobe		
Tennis Frock	4s	11d	Grey Trousers	4s	11d
Hat	1s		Shirt with		
Blazer	4s	11d	two Collars	4s	11d
Stockings	2s	11d	Tie	1s	11d
Shoes	2s	6d	Gloves	1s	6d
Princess slip	1s	11d	Socks	1s	6d
Knickers	1s	11d	Slipover	4s	11d
Total	£1 0s	1d	Total		19s 8d

An M & S account book of the 1930s and (right) the items of wardrobe acquired by 'Mrs Goodwife' and her husband (*see text*).

Goodwife was given £1 to spend by her husband – all that he could afford – to buy 'frock, hat, underclothes and shoes' and for £1 0s 1d she bought the wardrobe listed at left on the opposite page.

Despite the extra penny she had spent, her husband was so impressed that he gave her another £2 to buy clothes for the children and 'an outfit for our little girl who was going to school after the summer holidays'. Once again she was so successful in her shopping that this time her husband, 'not to be outdone by the smartness of his family', went himself to M & S to buy some clothes.

In fact, the husband saw so many varieties of shirts at M & S that he did not know which to buy, and in the end he settled for woven poplin. For 19s 8d he acquired the wardrobe listed at right on the opposite page.

M & S model customers of the 1930s were already behaving in a completely different way from Rowntree's victim families of the 1890s, and by 1939 it was being claimed that over 300 million separate purchases were being made by M & S customers in the course of a year. They were interested not only in 'marvellous value' but in more attractive clothes, more enterprising toys for the children (average family size had fallen, but expenditure on toys had risen), better household gadgets, and 'the garden beautiful' (bulbs were on sale at M & S stores). And they were obviously interested in better shopping facilities also. The Pantheon in Oxford Street certainly provided them. It advertised, for example, 'rails affixed to the top edge of the fruit counter which provide a handy resting place for customers' baskets' and 'a writing and rest room for customers' on the first floor – 'a notable departure for a fixed-price bazaar'.

Nonetheless, 'marvellous value' still mattered a good deal, as is shown by the enrolment of customers during the 1930s in the M & S savings clubs, organised by club leaders or agents, who collected contributions. Reading and Eastbourne were the first two centres, and when it was demonstrated by 1934 that turnover could be increased by this hire-purchase system, M & S spread the idea (which was already fashionable with other retailers, including department stores) and a Weekly Clubs Department was set up in 1935.

The club business increased enormously in popularity during the 1930s, as the figures of club receipts shown in the diagram *(right)* indicate.

The figures would have been much higher in 1939 if club trading had not been restricted as a result of the war.

This was the kind of business, however, which had more than financial ramifications: it encouraged customers to go into the M & S stores and examine what was on offer, and one reason why it flourished was that such direct access was far more revealing than skimming through the pages of a club catalogue, as members of mail-order clubs had to do.

During the Second World War, the range of goods available in the shops declined so that the proportion of personal incomes spent on goods and services fell to the exceptionally low figure of 68% in 1944. And yet, following air raids, members of the public are said to have shown 'increased interest in shopping'. At the same time there was often an acute shortage of food locally available for sale. The Bath store made effective use of nearby suppliers, one Bristol firm which

Below: Weekly Clubs Department receipts during the 1930s.

1939	£2,990,347
1938	£2,107,213
1937	£1,434,187
1936	£842,000
1935	£617,348

CLUB SHAREHOLDER'S CARD

PLEASE NOTE

Our Club Organisers carry an official Club-holder's Card, and no payment should be made unless that authority is produced.

WHEN THIS CLUB EXPIRES PLEASE JOIN AGAIN

had provided loaves for sandwiches now delivering the biggest bread load ever received – 700 quarters on one Monday afternoon. At Hastings stock was bought in from Tunbridge Wells, while at Portsmouth, where on one occasion there was no fresh water, heating or electricity, there was an increased demand for tea, coffee and snacks at the café bar.

Austerity persisted after 1945 so that customers still found themselves queuing to buy food and having to restrict their purchases of clothes. Yet for the first time they were thinking of themselves as one class of 'customers', whatever their social background. The 'New Look' of 1947 appealed to every class: the long jackets and tight trousers of the 'teddy boy' had upper-class Edwardian origins.

Discriminating people of all classes were prepared to look for the best food, not for the most expensive. Thus, Rebecca West, in 'Notes by the Way' in the now-defunct weekly *Time and Tide* in 1952, after comparing ham sandwiches in London, most of which she found unsatisfactory, 'not a necessary consequence of our national difficulties', turned happily to 'Messrs Marks and Spencer, who sell me a handsome ham sandwich for the astonishing sum of sixpence'.

The development of the 'welfare state' itself, it was often argued, was responsible for the changes, a view advanced by Lawrence Thompson of the *News Chronicle* (now also defunct) in 1955:

> 'Before the Welfare State there were broadly two classes of consumers, the middle class, who had the money, and the working class who hadn't. Now there is only one class; and I am told…that many a débutante wears an M & S nylon slip beneath her Dior dress as if she were just a Gateshead factory girl'.

(J. B. Priestley had written in 1934 of factory girls beginning to look like waitresses – but he had not claimed that they looked like débutantes.)

In 1954 and 1955, on the eve of the great expansion in the distribution of consumer goods, many statistical comparisons were being made between the habits of the customers of the early 1950s, emerging from the age of austerity, and the customers of the late 1930s, waiting, though they did not always know it, for war. Food consumption had increased from 29% to 32.3% of consumer expenditure, and housing (with rent controls) was down from 11.7% to 8.2%. Not all the prophecies as to how customers would behave when the shops were full again were to be realised. Food sales, which had increased by 39% between 1950 and 1954, were generally expected to hold up, but there was little recognition that clothing and footwear sales, which had increased by only 6%, would go through a boom. A London Press Exchange paper on *Shops and Shopping* in 1955 predicted that there would 'probably be an increase in the demand for durable consumer goods and a relative decline in textiles and clothing'. And that was only one year before Mary Quant opened her first new fashion shop.

In fact, the 'new generation', influenced by educational changes and new developments in the media, was to reveal an exceptional interest in clothes, first on the part of women, then of men. It was also to have enough money to spend on them. In 1938, according to a Ministry of Labour survey, boys between the ages of 15 and 20 who were at work had earned an average of 26s a week and girls 24s. In 1958 the comparable rates were £5 12s and £5 6s. The real earnings of both sexes had increased at double the rate of adults. In 1965 their expenditure

Below: Grainger Market, Newcastle-upon-Tyne – a painting of the store in *c.* 1895 and a photograph taken in 1953.

patterns showed that boys were spending 12s a week and girls 20s a week on clothes. Boys spent 13s on meals and snacks out, and girls 4s.

Meanwhile, there were changes in food habits – often inspired by holidays abroad – which were to transform M & S customers of the future. Already by 1956, as John Burnet has pointed out in his *Plenty and Want*, demand for foods formerly in cheap supply – meat, fat, sugar, eggs, tinned fruits and so on – had largely been satisfied, and customers were more concerned 'to improve the palatability' of their diet than to increase the quantity.

Not that M & S customers ever lost sight of the price factor, even when London was at its most 'swinging' during the 1960s. 'It's silly to buy other shoes, when I can buy these for 25s', said a Mayfair secretary in 1967, when trying on a pair of patent casuals at the M & S Marble Arch store.

In 1970, in a paper to the Chairman, Jan de Somogyi predicted the reactions of 'customers in the seventies'. There would be a change in age patterns with a larger proportion of customers in the under-25 and over-65 age groups. 'The increasingly affluent consumer (and he did not touch on the unemployed) demands a much faster rate of innovation in fabric, style, design and colour. This calls for a flexible production and distribution system: good communications and careful probing'. 'Good values', he added, 'are essential if clothing is to compete with the attractions of other ways of spending money... but these competitors also generate their own demand for a variety of new specialised garments – predominantly with the emphasis on comfort'.

Electronic check-out equipment in the Food Department at Edmonton.

Such sophisticated analysis of consumer habits was a feature of the 1960s and 1970s, when the identification of 'consumer profiles' became a necessary element in good marketing. It became the practice then to classify customers in terms of age, sex, marital status, 'social grade' and occupation, and to determine which groups bought most. Shares of 'sales value' could then be calculated. Thus, market research showed in the summer of 1979 that 82.7% of the buyers of one line in women's dresses at M & S were married, while for another line the figure was only 65.4%, and that as many as 32% of the customers for one line of dresses – and for blouses – were from professional and clerical occupations. For women's tailored jackets, however, 28.3% of the customers were factory workers. Such analysis showed that M & S was increasingly servicing the whole social spectrum, if not the whole age range. Thus, when the Kensington High Street (London) store was opened in 1977, it was expected that it would appeal not only, like Marble Arch, to tourists – they were expected to be about a third of the customers – but (in the words of an evening paper) to 'the many wealthy and titled residents of Kensington and Chelsea'.

It was during this most recent period of M & S history that it acquired a whole group of new customers abroad, whose habits could be contrasted with those of the English. Canadian habits in a scattered continent seemed to be very different from those in Britain. As for the French, it was quickly perceived that they were looking for the goods they crossed the Channel to buy in M & S stores in Britain: the range of goods on sale in Paris includes favourites like traditional British cashmere pullovers, Shetland sweaters and pure wool skirts, coats and kilts along with British 'specialty foods', like rich fruit cake, matured cheddar cheese, jams, marmalade, spiced fruit buns and – of course – tea.

RECEPTION AREA AT MICHAEL HOUSE, 47 BAKER STREET – M & S HEADQUARTERS SINCE 1958

MANAGEMENT

At Michael House in Baker Street there is an imposing board room – with portraits on the wall of Simon Marks, Edward Sieff, and Marcus Sieff. There is also a copy of the M & S coat of arms, designed in 1968, in which a lion, representing England, and an owl, representing wisdom, support a symbol of the Archangel Michael. A pair of golden scales portrays justice (and fair trading), white roses represent Yorkshire, where Michael Marks had his first stall, a ladder (from Jacob's dream) is a sign of the aspiration and will to improve, and a horn of plenty stands for the plenitude of goods sold by the company. Beneath the crest is the company's motto, 'Strive, Probe, Apply'.

The coat of arms marks the acceptance of M & S as a national institution. There is also a pendulum clock in the board room which was presented to M & S by the Albert Martin Holding Company in 1978 to celebrate 50 years of business association. It leaves no doubt about its message: 'Time Marches On'.

In the earliest days of Marks without Spencer, all management was Michael Marks management, but he soon found that he needed helpers. His first male employee, William F. Norris, met him one year before the M & S partnership began, and was described in 1903, when M & S became a company, as Acting Secretary and Manager of the Derby Street warehouse at Manchester. In 1903 he had one share, in 1906 90 more, in 1907 another two. He seems also to have been responsible for much of the buying. In 1914 his salary was £220 a year, and in 1915 he was William Chapman's nominee for a directorship of the Company, but he attended only one meeting before Simon Marks's reorganisation of the business. He died in 1920.

It was a sign of M & S continuity that his son Wilfred joined the business in 1924 and served M & S loyally and diligently for many years. He worked at first on the distribution of goods from the company's warehouses, then on toys and fancy goods, then on 'enamelware, crockery, glass, Dutch bulbs and gramophone records', served for a time as assistant to Israel Sieff, moved to store management in Blackpool and Manchester, returned to textiles, became an alternate director in 1940 and a full director in 1950, and ended as Assistant Managing Director in 1963, a position which he held until his retirement in 1971.

Long after Michael Marks and Tom Spencer had worked together informally before 1903, with few pieces of paper to record what they were doing, Simon Marks and Israel Sieff shared one room in Chiswell Street, where they 'never stopped talking about business', discussing how, in Israel's words 'our business dealings could incorporate the ideals which had been taught us by our parents'.

The family sense was crucial, as is shown at every point in this history. And it can be illustrated at the top management level by not only the Sieffs but also the

William F. Norris, Michael Marks's first male employee, who was Acting Secretary when M & S became a limited-liability company in 1903.

81

Above: Harry Sacher, a Director from 1932 to 1962. He was the husband of Miriam Marks, daughter of the founder of M & S.

Below: Bruce Goodman, Joint Managing Director from 1967 to 1971.

Sachers – Harry and Michael, the latter Vice-Chairman until 1984, who joined the business in 1938 and, after serving as Group Merchandise Manager, became an alternate director in 1954 and a full director in 1961. As a grandson of Michael Marks, he is part of the core tradition. Because of such links the formal hierarchy of M & S has never been divorced from the informal relationships which cut through the hierarchies. When Pamela Bradney wrote an Oxford doctoral thesis on 'Welfare and Tradition in Stores' in 1957, having worked for a time in M & S (as a kind of anthropologist), two of the main points she made were, first, that the business was still a family business and, second, that the board was in a way 'in continuous session'.

Of course, the board by then included members outside the first ring of families, and formal meetings of the full board, which by 1952 included the Company Secretary and 10 other directors, were held regularly to review progress and to decide policies.

In the beginning, before 1903, there was, of course, no board. Nor were there any minutes of meetings. There are, however, jottings of figures, showing that the control of management was mainly financial. The sales staff who served at the market stalls or, later, at the penny bazaars were appointed locally and served on local terms. No business, indeed, could have been managed more simply than was M & S in the earliest years of its growth. And when in 1956, after turnover was well past the £100,000,000 mark and there seemed to be signs of increasing rigidity within a huge and still-expanding structure, drastic steps were immediately taken to simplify all over again. 'Operation Simplification', as it was called, followed by a 'good-housekeeping campaign', ushered in the M & S of the late-twentieth century as it still exists.

B.W. Goodman, who was Secretary of M & S at the time – he had joined M & S at its Kilburn store in 1932 – carefully described why and how the streamlining operation began. 'Growth was not confined to sales and profits alone', he explained. 'Overheads were growing even faster, so that profits before tax expressed as a percentage of turnover were being steadily eroded from 10½% in 1945-1946 to 8½% in 1955-56. We were determined not to join the annual lament of Company Chairmen about the rising operating and overhead costs. Instead, we resolved to take a positive, even drastic action to arrest and reverse the trend'. The operation began properly with a communications exercise: all members of the staff were told what was to happen. An enormous amount of M & S paper was decreed superfluous – a documentation exhibition was to be held later to demonstrate just how much – and systems which had lasted for decades disappeared overnight. For example, booking in of goods at stores ceased to be a detailed procedure involving a description of all articles received. Nor did stores require invoices for merchandise from suppliers, while sales girls were no longer expected to fill in forms when they required goods from the stockroom. Nor were store managers required to submit long weekly reports to head office.

The immediate effects of the change were striking: a drastic cut in the volume of paper, a cut in the number of store office staff by half, a sharp reduction in store and head office costs, and a passing on of price reductions to customers. More important still, the fostering of a new outlook inside the business meant that 'Operation Simplification' never came to an end. Thus in 1984, no form used in the business was reprinted before it had been 'assessed for function'. Simplification became part of the M & S approach to management and was extended to other areas besides paper. In 1977 it was reported that nearly £4 million had been saved during the previous four years in gas and electricity – in a 'turn off' and 'switch off' campaign supervised by the company's Chief Engineer, Bernard Lubert. 'Watt-watching' had become a new M & S pastime. Yet such continuing campaigns were seen not as economy drives but positively as drives for more effective use of resources.

Without 'Operation Simplification' and its successors, profit margins would have contracted. Without it M & S would never have established its reputation as a model organisation. It would certainly not have had quite the same allure. 'Keep it simple' remains a managerial maxim.

The organisational history of M & S cannot be quite as easily simplified as its internal business records. Indeed, the absence rather than abundance of documentation creates difficulties for the historian. The first filing system was apparently inaugurated in February 1919 and was thereafter 'adopted by the various departments', but it is difficult to trace the development of different departments and of the names of people in charge of them during the 1920s and 1930s. Much of the history of M & S has to be told, rather like pre-history, on the evidence of things rather than words.

The first bazaars employed few staff, and these were usually recruited locally and on local terms. Yet Michael Marks and Tom Spencer knew that all staff required

Above: 'Operation Simplification', 1956 – paperwork representing one week's invoices before and after the campaign got into its stride.

Left: Accounts Office at the Pantheon store, Oxford Street, in 1938. Standing in the centre is Mr L. Richman, the store manager.

supervision. It has been recalled that at Hull, Tom Spencer and his wife once dropped into the bazaar and found one sales assistant 'doing' another assistant's hair. The assistants did not know them and when Spencer asked to be served, one of the girls said 'Ark at 'im'. Spencer promptly sacked the lot and took over with his wife until new staff could be recruited. Spencer had been responsible, too, for the warehousing side, which by 1910 was more systematically organised. It was in that year that the Birmingham depot was opened in Birchall Street 'for receiving and forwarding goods manufactured in and around Birmingham', and a catalogue of all the goods stocked by the company was issued 'for the use of Branches and Travelling Inspectors'.

It is possible to form a picture of William Chapman as a manager at this time and of his contribution to the history of M & S: there are surviving documents, particularly an affidavit of 1916, in which he describes his activities over the previous few years. He had (he writes) regularly devoted at least one and sometimes three days a week to M & S affairs, and in the latter half of 1915 had visited 40 branches. Since 1912 (he goes on) all negotiations for and completions of leases had passed through his hands, and he had been 'entirely responsible for the general finance and the preparation of stock accounts'. Indeed, going back further still, since he joined the board he had 'entirely reorganised the whole system of business of the Company in relation to the keeping of its accounts, control of its branches, checking of losses and deficiencies on goods, and opening of new warehouse depots'.

It was under Chapman, indeed, that M & S management first became more sophisticated. On Michael Marks's death a team of inspectors had been appointed, headed at first by his friend Carl Jacobson. The inspectors were expected to keep an eye both on bazaar operations and on leasehold arrangements. In November 1908, for instance, McQuillan had to deal with the problem of why, in Swansea, M & S had to close daily at certain fixed hours while 'our competitors seem to be immune from these restrictions'.

Wages at the different bazaars do not seem to have been discussed at board meetings before February 1909, when several lists were 'noted for investigation'. The most frequent item on the board's agenda, other than the acquisition of properties, related to 'deficiencies of stock' in the bazaars. In October 1908, for example, it was decided to send letters to bazaar managers in Birkenhead, Bath, Birmingham, Croydon, Harrogate, Newport, Leicester, Reading, Stockton, Swansea and Southwark (London), where there was a deficiency of more than 3%. 'We must ask you', the letter read, 'to exercise special vigilance and care with regard to (your stock) and trust the next report will be more favourable'. Blackpool and Worcester were soon added to the list. Weekly reports were sent in from the 'branches', as they began to be thought of, and in April 1909 it was suggested that they should always be sent in to arrive in Manchester by Monday.

By 1913 M & S had divided the country into 'grounds', and the inspectors were beginning to be called supervisors, while above them the three directors were taking responsibility for store supervision, each with a third of the stores to watch over. There was also a specialised group of 'stocktakers' who reported to the supervisors – two of them were mentioned as early as 1901, and in 1903 a third was added – and in the light of experience in September 1909 the board concluded first that 'women as stocktakers would be more adaptable than men'.

In the same year there was the first talk of training, when it was agreed that a number of assistants should be specially trained by Miss Gibbs, 'travelling manageress', with a view to installing them as manageresses 'when such vacancies occur'. Miss Gibbs, a remarkable woman who had served for part of her M & S career in London, was based thereafter at Oldham Street, Manchester, specifically for this purpose.

During the First World War the proportion of manageresses seems to have increased, but there were great difficulties in supervising the system. In July 1916, therefore, reorganisation of staff was discussed, mainly the further supervision of branches. This was followed by individual consultations with the supervisors, and a supervisors' conference, the first of many, was held in February 1917. By 1919 the country was formally divided into 12 areas (or 'spheres'), each with its own supervisor and its own stocktaker.

The board itself became more specialised, and at a meeting in March 1916 the directors allocated their duties departmentally. Chapman accepted supervision of finance, leases, properties and building plans, Simon Marks undertook to carry out buying in Manchester and London, to supervise the London and suburban branches and to engage in 'prospecting', and Thomas Spencer junior agreed 'to take over the buying for Birmingham – "assisted if necessary by Mr Marks" – and to supervise all other Branches and prospecting'. When Israel Sieff joined the board he was not given specific responsibilities but was told to offer his services 'at any time whenever possible'.

The managerial system of M & S open bazaars took time to establish itself on the spot, and it was not until the 1920s that a system was introduced whereby floorwalkers examined counters, goods, tills and standards of service. (Annual revisions of salaries and wages date back to 1912, but it was not until more than 20 years later that there was the first serious talk of a Personnel Department.) In 1927 William McQuillan had been designated Superintendent, and the area supervisors included five women, but it was left to the directors to explain to the managers – who were beginning to outnumber the manageresses – their role in the developing organisation. A letter of 1926 survives, written by Sieff to J. Abbott, a store manager, enclosing a Christmas gift of £15 and telling him that his salary would be increased to £8 as from 1 January 1927. 'We feel sure', Israel wrote, 'that this increase will be the means of bringing home to you the fact that better results in our stores can be attained only by serious thought and constant application of the principles which govern our business. We further wish you to realise that the Directors are watching your career in the service of the Company, and that promotion and improved position in the Company will be the reward of your wholehearted cooperation'.

Managers might have problems with the authorities as well as their staff, for as late as the 1930s there were critics of the 'new methods of shopkeeping' who believed that stores like M & S were putting temptation into the way of people going into them. Among them was Claude Mullins, a well-known and controversial London magistrate, who bound over a number of people accused of shoplifting from the M & S store at Brixton on the grounds that in open stores 'temptation was being placed in the way of thousands and thousands of people'. By then the Brixton store had 12 island counters, each staffed by two assistants, and it was estimated that about 20,000 people were visiting it every week.

Below: The staff rest room at a store today and (below right) its equivalent in 1938. Right: The staff washroom at the Pantheon, Oxford Street, in 1938. Far right: The dental surgery at Michael House.

Above: Flora Solomon (seen here with Lord Sieff in 1983) was invited by Simon Marks to help organise M & S's personnel department and welfare schemes after they had met for the first time at a dinner party in 1934.

The largest open-display stores before the Second World War were employing very large numbers of staff, with total M & S staff reaching the 18,000 mark and with 16 stores with more than 1,600 feet of counter space. The Pantheon had a staff of nearly 300, under a manager, a deputy manager, and several departmental managers, and it included a staff manageress responsible for welfare and training. It was the development of this last office which was to become an M & S hallmark, although the directors of the company continued to interest themselves in all aspects of welfare and training to a degree unusual in such a large business.

The creation of a special Personnel Department in 1934 was a landmark in the history of M & S. It was headed by a remarkable woman, Mrs Flora Solomon, who was attracted into business employment for the first time in an exciting and many-sided life which had begun in Tsarist Russia. In 1933 a consulting Medical Officer had been appointed as a prelude to the establishment of a comprehensive medical (and later a dental) service. It was in this same year that Marks first used the term 'welfare' in his address to the shareholders. A new Welfare Committee headed by Mrs Solomon met – and it still meets – each week to consider individual personal problems referred to it.

'Management Without Tears' was the title of an article written in *Sparks* by Mrs Solomon, who pointed not only to the 'material provisions' of welfare schemes but to the psychology of working at M & S. The word 'well-being', she said, required analysing, 'for sometimes people assume that it can be achieved by good material conditions alone'. But in the last resort 'one gets a real satisfaction out of doing work well, and…training for the job is an essential part of any welfare scheme'.

And so it was in M & S, where a new training scheme was introduced in 1934 at the same time as the Personnel Department was set up. Training by stages became the objective – and it was training not only to enhance individual job satisfaction but to encourage a sense of working in a team. 'A store is not a collection of private individuals', Mrs Solomon insisted, 'but a team of people working for a common object… The well-being of an individual cannot exist in a vacuum'. For her, staff manageresses were key people in the welfare scheme. They were most effective when they administered 'their welfare work not as something "tacked on" to the business organisation, but as an integral part of it'.

Every member of M & S staff was made to feel a member of an organisation directly concerned with his or her welfare. 'We now employ one of the largest retail sales forces in the country', Marks told the shareholders in 1934, 'and it is the constant concern of the board to improve conditions of employment. We have instituted a fair scale of remuneration for all grades and categories of our staff which provides for progressive increases in salary, having regard to age, length of service and ability. Our Welfare Department is actively engaged in studying and ministering to the personal needs of our employees… It has organised a range of services, medical, athletic and social, which has gone far to stimulate a team spirit, a welcome development in any business organisation'.

One of the first two Joint Personnel Managers was Frank Ross, who worked in the Personnel Department until his retirement in 1965. He had joined M & S in 1920 in the stocktaking department and by 1927 had become a lone accountant travelling round the stores seeking to establish a unified clerical system. From

that work the External Administration Department was to evolve, but after 1934 Ross was concerned with human stocktaking and accounting. It is largely on the basis of his own collected papers that it is possible to recapture the spirit in which the Personnel Department operated during the 1930s, linking welfare, training and administration in a pioneering way unfamiliar in retailing – an occupation which did not have a conspicuously good record in staffing conditions.

The nineteenth-century retailing story had been one of long hours, low pay and uneasy, often unpleasant, human relations. The new M & S policies were in dramatic contrast. They turned retailing into a model occupation – with new facilities, like the canteen (later to be called the restaurant), and the rest room. By 1962 an American writer, S.J. Goldsmith, observed, 'If Britain is a welfare state, M & S is a welfare organisation within the welfare state. Their scores of thousands of employees used to be looked after well during their working days, in old age and in sickness long before the welfare state came into being... This way of running a joint business is known as "Marks and Spencer economics"'. And since that date, 1962, while the benefits of the welfare state have been cut, those of M & S have been increased. 'Every single thing that we've done because we felt we had a moral obligation', the present Lord Sieff has pointed out, 'has also, within five or ten years, turned out to be good business.' Almost £60 million a year is now spent on bonuses, non-contributory pensions, subsidised meals, health care and other staff services.

An element of stronger central direction is noticeable in the company after 1934. All advertisements for staff, for example, had to go through the Personnel Department, and wages and conditions of work, as well as training, were considered as part of 'welfare'. At the same time a greater central interest was shown in the 'grass-roots' of M & S. In 1934, a 'Suggestions Scheme' was introduced – 'so many were sent in', it was stated in January 1935, that it would take 'two or three weeks to examine them properly' – and a year later two additional welfare schemes were introduced. The first was a pension scheme for senior men in the business, a scheme which was progressively widened and improved later, with M & S contributing an increasing proportion of the cost until eventually the scheme became non-contributory; the second was the Marks and Spencer Benevolent Trust, endowed by Simon Marks and the family, which provided retirement benefits for those outside the pension scheme.

The object of both schemes was to protect the employee against the sense of fear and insecurity. They were necessary counterparts, therefore, to the efficiency policies to which M & S was also committed, seeking to induce in the employee the feeling that in his working life he was 'not at the mercy of impersonal forces', and that he would have the chance to specialise and progress. Career opportunities began to be identified. 'There is a great variety of posts open to women in our employment', applicants were told, 'and in practice the vast majority of vacancies in the higher ranks are filled from people in the lower ranks. Among our women as well as our men employees there is a real career open to those who possess initiative and ability'.

The war increased the number of welfare problems and made it impossible to continue to develop training as had been hoped, but the Personnel Department was determined after the war to carry out further welfare schemes. Its Annual Report in 1953 was a lengthy and thorough document which began with 'store management' and ended with the work of the Personnel Committee. There was a

Gramophone records were a popular item in M & S stores in the 1930s and for a time were sold under the company's own label.

challenge, the report suggested. 'The next five years are vital for the build-up of our management reserve, as in that period we have the lowest number of retirements under normal conditions, namely 13. Between 1959 and 1964 we must anticipate 45 retirements if the present service age limit of 60 is maintained'.

The challenge was met, for it was between 1959 and 1964 that M & S was transformed into the remarkable company that Simon Marks bequeathed to his successors. He himself had posed a number of leading questions in a series of notes drafted in 1954, called 'Thinking About the Business'. 'Are we following our principles of production and merchandising?' was the first. 'Do we understand them sufficiently or are we merely paying lip service to them?' was the second. 'Are we at Head Office too remote from the Stores?' and 'Are the Departments too remote from one another?' were third. The thirteenth was 'How can we educate our personnel in the spirit and the philosophy of our business?' – a major theme dealt with in the last chapter of this book – and the sixteenth and seventeenth were 'Do we appreciate the work of our Personnel Department – how the appointments are made and how the careers of these new men are followed up?' and 'Are we acquainted with the work of our Welfare and Educational organisation? Its impact upon the smooth working of our staff?'

By the mid-1960s M & S organisation was geared both to providing improved consumer services and to facilitating further expansion. At the centre – and major decisions were taken centrally – there were the key groups in the buying process. The selectors chose the lines, the merchandisers determined quantities to be bought, and the heads of department exercised control over both. At the final

Left: The staff gym at Michael House.

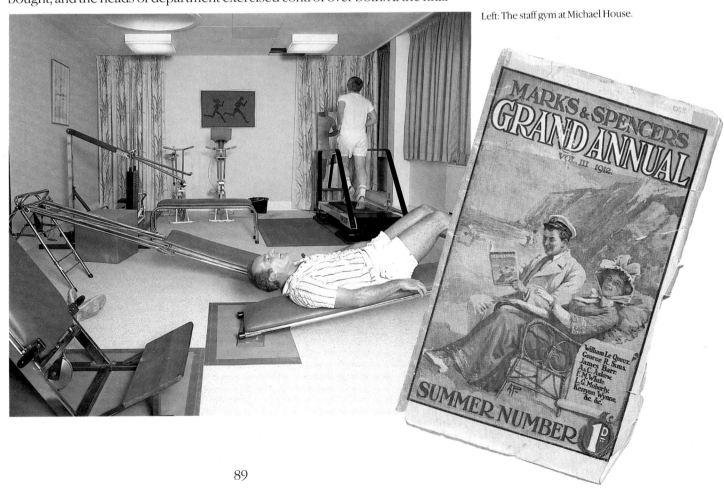

A corner of a computer room at Michael House.

stage, one of the higher executives or one of the directors participated also, but they could intervene at other points in the process, too.

At the store level, the characteristic large staff structure consisted of a manager, assistant manager, a staff manageress, two or three departmental managers (along with management trainees), six or seven supervisors, a warehouse manager, a cashier, and about 100 general staff working on the sales floor and in the stockrooms, offices and staff quarters. In some stores, however, there was a far smaller establishment and the manager had to carry out most of the management tasks himself. There was always a staff manageress, however, with a prime responsibility for the welfare of the staff, including their selection, training, deployment and development. About two-thirds of the staff manageresses were then being promoted from supervisory jobs within the store, while the remaining third were a direct intake from the universities or from outside M & S.

The manager's job was well described in a paper of 1967, prepared after consultation between H.B. Freeman and the managers of the Pantheon, Aberdeen, Colchester, Preston, Leicester, Guildford and Southend stores. It began, not with the finished product, but with induction and training (one in five entrants had a university background) and dwelt on the subsequent team aspects of the job as well as with the manager's distinctive role. 'A man is selected for management training', the paper began, 'because he has a positive personality, and qualities of intelligence, leadership and enthusiasm. His training over a period of years is aimed at giving him understanding of the philosophy and principles on which the business is based, as well as detailed knowledge of the systems and methods we use'.

Once initially trained, store managers were 'people who should make things happen in the best way to arrive at desired objectives'. A manager was encouraged from the start to be self-reliant and have a 'critical approach to his job', and he was expected to be mobile. 'Promotion is gained by climbing the ladder on merit and ability, and not waiting in the lift to be taken automatically to the next level'.

Managers received guidance from divisional superintendents, of which there were 12, each responsible, as in the past, for the supervision of a group of stores. Each division had its own economic and social characteristics. There were periodic meetings within the divisions of managers and trainees, and there were regular meetings of divisional superintendents. There were also visits to suppliers.

M & S kept good personal records and in 1984 the Personnel Department had a staff of 900 trained people looking after the needs of a staff of almost 50,000 people from their induction to their retirement. Indeed, individual needs continued to be met after retirement. All permanent full-time and part-time staff automatically become members of the pensions scheme administered by a separate trust company: it provides benefits so far in excess of the state pension scheme that M & S contracted out, and over £291.5 million was spent in 1983/4 on salaries and wages, pensions, staff welfare and profit sharing.

Given the roundedness of the M & S managerial system, it is interesting to set out a list of questions about the future similar to those which Simon Marks posed 30 years ago in his paper 'Thinking About the Business'. Already the increased size of the enterprise has brought about developments which were not anticipated then or in 1934. One of them is the growth of computerisation, and this has so far been handled inside M & S in a relatively conservative way, although automation (with or without computers) has revolutionised the production processes of some of the M & S suppliers. It was not until 1976, however, that M & S acquired its own computer, with a staff of 54, which is now used for central accounting and audit purposes. The textile distribution system is only partly computerised even today, and there is no commitment to point-of-sale 'data capture'. There is also a healthy fear of the amount of paper a computer can spawn.

Another change inside M & S has been of a very different kind: the setting up of 'communication groups'. Such groups were first formed during the mid-1970s, but in 1983 important modifications were made in an effort to make the groups more effective. Each group was to be chaired by a member of staff – a two-day training course for these was planned – and each group would start its meeting without 'management' being present. 'The main aim of the extended schemes', said Carole Watson, the Communication Manager, was 'to increase staff participation in both the meeting and its organisation'.

One of several sophisticated new types of electronic till under trial in 1984.

To what extent would computers and communications figure on a new list of questions? Certainly store design and changing customer attitudes and preferences would be important lines of questioning. Credit cards? Self-service? Delivery services? Access by car to stores? (This has already been greatly improved.) New product ranges? It is a time for questioning, as a new phase in M & S history opens. The success of the answers will depend, as in the past, on the capacity of M & S staff to implement them not only effectively but willingly and with zest. And if only for that reason there is no more important chapter in this book than that which follows on the history of M & S staff in a century of change.

STAFF AT BISHOP AUCKLAND STORE IN 1928

STAFF

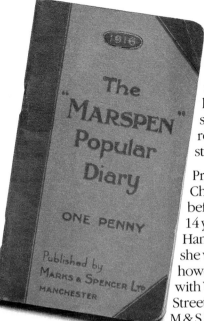

The best source for the story of M & S staff is the personal reminiscences of members of the staff themselves, what have been called 'old timers' tales'. There are other sources, however, including the *Staff Bulletin*, which revealed in 1947 that there were still seven members of the staff who had been with M & S since before 1918.

Pride of place in staff history goes to Esther Brown (later Mrs Chrimes), who joined Michael Marks in 1893 – one year before the beginning of the M & S partnership. She was then 14 years old and her first responsibilities were to assist Hannah Marks with the bringing up of the Marks family. At first she worked on the market stall only on Saturdays. Later, however, she crossed the Pennines to Manchester and worked with William Norris, the first male employee, at the Robert Street warehouse. Eventually she graduated fully within the M & S business, serving as manageress of Oldham Street, Manchester, until she left in 1911. (The first joint manageresses at Oldham Street were Ada and Gertie Probert, and another early member of staff was Laura Cowburn.) Esther Brown soon afterwards emigrated to Australia, but returned to Britain just before the Second World War. In 1964 M & S, hearing that she was seriously ill in hospital in Manchester, tracked her down and provided her with a pension and flat. She died seven years later at the age of 91.

Life in the Oldham Street store before 1914 is reasonably well documented. In 1909 the board decided to advertise in the *Manchester Guardian* for a young woman to train as manageress under Miss Gibbs. Mrs Kelly, the successful applicant, was paid the relatively low wage of 15s a week, plus a commission on sales. The idea of commission, which was never to figure prominently in the history of M & S, was quietly dropped, and her wage increased first to 30s and then by annual increments of 5s a week (with a Christmas bonus of £5).

During this period Mrs Kelly was assisted by a 'first girl' and 10 assistants. She engaged staff herself, acted as cashier, ordered goods from the warehouse, and checked stock as it came in and at the end of the week. At the age of 15 or 16, straight from school, assistants received from 4s up to 18s a week. There were Christmas bonuses according to length of service.

Hours were long – on Saturdays up to 10 pm – and it was not until 1912 that a statutory half-day holiday was introduced. The manageress had a fortnight's holiday with pay, however, and the assistants a week's. There was a 10-minute break for cocoa in the morning and an hour off for lunch. There were no special uniforms, but girls were expected to dress tidily and in dark clothes. 'When lemon cheese samples were exhibited', Mrs Kelly later recalled, 'the girls wore overalls and much stress was laid on the importance of clean hands'.

To be a shop assistant was a 'respectable' occupation for women in Edwardian times, and to be a warehouseman was to be in a position of trust. Yet wages were low and hours were long. Margaret Bondfield, a shop assistant who was to become the first woman to enter the Cabinet of a British government (in 1929), wrote an article on the subject of women's work in shops in the *Economic*

Notification of the commission earned by a manageress at Croydon store in November 1911.

Journal in 1899, where she referred to 1,000 shop assistants working a 63- to a 69-hour week in London's West End. A law of 1892 had laid it down that young people under 18 must not be employed in a shop for more than 74 hours a week, including meal times, and in 1904 (after strenuous efforts) a further law was passed that empowered local authorities to make an order fixing the hours at which shops must stop serving customers if a two thirds majority of shopkeepers agreed: these had to be not *earlier* than 7pm (or 1 o'clock on early-closing day).

Violet Humphries (later Mrs Pierce) recalled in 1959, when she was 75, how she applied to work at the Brixton store for 7s a week (with unspecified hours) in 1903. 'My father was furious', she added, 'and after a day or two insisted I gave in my notice. But "Our Miss Gibbs", the proprietor of the Bazaar in Fetter Lane, was able to talk mother on to my side, so that father, muttering observations that "he was nobody in this house", was obliged to give his grudging consent. When the day came for the new Bazaar to open (in 1903) there was a queue from the shop to the top of Atlantic Road into Brixton Road underneath the arches. We had a commissionaire to control the crowds, girls were fainting, people were shouting, it was a fantastic day…It was like a tube train during the rush hour, and it kept like that every Saturday'.

Sarah Bushell, who went to work on Saturdays in Grainger Market, Newcastle, in 1900, moved six years later to Scarborough Penny Bazaar; she left the business in 1913, when she got married. Another early sales assistant was Edith Puttley, who in 1959 recalled starting work at Brixton in 1903, when all the sales staff wore black, with the exception of the store manageress, who sported a white blouse. 'She had a small back room and popped her head out from time to time to see if there was too much noise'. Work began at 9am, with the six assistants serving ribbons, buttons, records, and toys – toys being Mrs Puttley's specialty. At morning break, coffee or tea was prepared on a small gas ring at the back of the store.

At Leeds, when Gertie Nicholson started work in 1906 at the age of 14 – working at first only on Tuesdays from midday to 8 pm and on Saturdays from midday to 10 pm for 3s 6d a week – only tea was provided at lunch-time and the girls took turns in going up a quarter of an hour beforehand to make it. They carried their own food with them, but had two canteen cookers for warming it up. The store consisted of eight sections on either side of the Cross Arcade, and Miss Nicholson soon graduated to full-time work at 7s 6d a week – working from Mondays to Fridays from 9 am to 8 pm and on Saturdays from 9 am to 10.30 pm.

On the warehousing side Walter Speer, who joined the City Road warehouse in 1910 and went on to serve M & S for fifty years, vividly recalled in 1961 the underground stockroom where 'incoming deliveries were made from the street, down a wooden chute through trap doors in the pavement'. It was his job to load goods as they were received into the lift and bring them up from the basement to the first floor, where the packers made up cases for the sales floor.

Considerable attention was paid to staffing matters during the First World War, when retail wages did not rise as much as prices and when store management was far from straightforward. There are few surviving accounts of what it was like to manage a store at that time. There is a reference in Board Minutes, however, in March 1916 to a decision to advertise for 'a first class buyer for Haberdashery, Hardware and all kinds of cheap fancy goods made in Birmingham and district,

Mr Marks and Mr Spencer to interview suitable applicants'. Only Marks appears to have done any interviewing, and a few weeks later he reported that no one was suitable.

In 1917 the wages of manageresses in training ranged from as little as 20s a week to 27s 6d, and those of a stock-keeper from 15s to 25s. There was a successful strike at the Army and Navy stores in London just after the end of the war which directed public attention to the whole subject of wages and hours, but it seems to have had no repercussions for M & S. For the early 1920s, the best source for M & S staffing policy is the record of speeches made by Simon Marks at the London staff dinners. 'We see the same faces year after year', Simon told his dinner audience in 1923, 'and I feel with some justification it surely means that people like us and like to remain our servants. I think, so far as length of service is concerned, our firm would compare most favourably with any other firm in the country'. 'It is extraordinary', he went on, 'how the ladies, in particular, are adapting themselves to the new ideas and the new order of things'. It was in the same vein that in 1928 Marks described 'the enthusiasm, devotion and energy' of the M & S staff as 'one of the main assets of the business'. In 1921 there had been an additional note with what is now a topical ring. 'In other trades', Simon Marks told his staff, 'there is great unemployment. We try – in fact, we have made it "a duty" – to keep on as many (people) as possible. There are many Branches which we might have closed with profit, but we preferred to keep them going, and so not add to the unemployment'. Unemployment was to remain a disturbing feature of the inter-war years: it never fell below 1 million. Yet the M & S staff grew continuously – both locally and at head office.

It was not all work and no play, however. During the 1930s the range of 'social activities' was to widen, but there was to be no radical change. The reminiscences of retiring staff do not rigidly separate out work from lesiure. To be a member of M & S staff was to share in a way of life.

In this spirit E. Tolson recalled the early days when she worked at the Church Street store in Blackpool. She started there in June 1923, when there were only three island counters along with 'a small room used as a canteen, with one toilet in one corner... There was no cloakroom, only a passage with a few hooks leading to the canteen. We only had one porter', she went on, and 'no lift, all goods had to be carried upstairs by the staff. Being a seaside store, we were busier in the season than at Christmas. Being cashier involved more duties, signing all carters' sheets, invoices, and all general office work'. There were no bank safes, so she 'used to hide money in teapots, jugs, chambers, pans etc'.

'At Christmas time, we had 60 parcels from Derby Street warehouse, we had a Father Christmas which caused a lot of excitement. One day the manager was lost, during lunch break, but his hat and coat was still in the office, and walking round there he was discovered dressed as Father Christmas'.

In 1964 two people retired from the Bath store after 40 years' service with M & S. They both began work at Bath before the new store was complete, and they remembered the opening day as a major event in their own lives as well as in the life of a business. In the same year Sylvia Hill, floor supervisor at Bristol, who had started 40 years earlier with haberdashery, retired as supervisor of men's wear. (*En route* she had been a window dresser and a floor walker.) Margaret Sharp, who started at South Shields in 1924, first worked on the toy counter, where she

Recruitment brochures of the 1940s.

Staff pictures. Upper row, from left: Levenshulme, 1930 (closed 1938); Bridlington, 1923; unidentified roof-top group in the mid-1930s; North Road, Brighton, 1932. Lower row, from left: M & S Building Group members, about 1921; South Shields, 1920; Broad Street, Reading, 1912.

NEWBURY.—A ladies' Football Match was recently played between the Marks and Spencer team and Woodlands Laundry, and was won by M. & S. by two goals to one.

The M. & S. team looked very smart in their pale green shorts and blouses. After five minutes' play, Miss Valda Davis scored for M. & S. and right at the end of the game Miss Mary Byng shot the winning goal.

The event was so popular that the spectators crowded over the touchline into the field of play.

MARKET STREET, MANCHESTER.—The Table Tennis team, known as "The Quins," and consisting of the Misses O'Keefe, Jakum, Fink, and the two Garson sisters, recently beat the crack team of the Manchester Social Club and are now anxious to meet any M. & S. team.

Left: 1. The Stockton-on-Tees column. 2. M. and S. at the Colchester Carnival. Above: 1. Coventry in the country and (2) the manager finds the way. 3. Mr. Stephens on Birkenhead's first outing, twelve years ago. 4. Lewisham. 5. Sinehead Tennis section. 6. Wedding bells (and belles?) at York.

WESTON-SUPER-MARE.—M. and S. played a prominent part in the opening ceremony of the new open-air swimming pool at Weston-super-Mare. There were several mannequin parades, in which a number of M. & S. girls took part; and a fine challenge trophy was presented by the firm for the Ladies' Handicap Race. The affair went off very successfully before a big audience. A newsreel was taken, which is being shown in many cinemas throughout the country.

33

1. "Three Macks," Chester—at Scarborough. 2. "Before Breakfast," Ipswich—at Minehead. 3. Torquay on a Cruise. 4. The joys of supervising Douglas Store. 5. Tossing the Supervisor—Rhyl. 6. Two of Chelmsford's Bright Sparks.

Holiday snaps published in *Sparks*.

had 'the marathon job of removing an army of toy soldiers, dusting them and putting them back on parade daily'. 'Even then', she recalled in 1964 (a year before her death), 'we at M & S were dust-conscious'. Another of her duties was to help the assistant manageress lift and unpack crates in the back lane. 'It's no wonder that I acquired muscles like a boxer . . . In the summer season one of my additional duties was to stand at the front of the shop with a bag of money tied around my waist selling rock, buckets and spades. After three years a stockroom was built. I took sole charge and I am still there. What's more I am still shouting "Keep your fixtures tidy!".

Two others to complete 40 years' service in 1964 were George Challenger and Cecil Putt. The former had answered an advertisement, had been interviewed by F.M. Smith, Company Secretary, and had started at a salary of 30s a week. (Smith, by the way, was then paid £250 a year.) For a time Challenger had worked in the Finance Department with 'Julie' Kaye, where one of his duties was to buy foreign currency to pay for foreign purchases. In 1929 he had answered a company call for 'management material' and moved to Camden Town (London), later serving short spells in a three year period at East Ham (London), Hereford, Glasgow Argyll Street, Aldershot, Paisley and Barrow before joining head office as a merchandiser in men's underwear and finally moving to the lingerie group.

Cecil Putt, manager at Newton Abbot, had started work in 1924 at the old Derby Street warehouse in Manchester. 'I thought I would aim high', he recalled, 'and as the average wage for a youth of 18 in those days was around 30s I asked for 35s. You can imagine my delight when I was told, "Start on Monday and your wages will be £2 a week"'. When the warehouse closed he moved to Oldham Street, Manchester, then to Shrewsbury, York, Leeds, Bristol, Hereford, Wolverhampton, Bradford, Luton, Leicester, Marble Arch, Nottingham, Bournemouth, Portsmouth, Middlesbrough, Derby, Poole, Taunton, Torquay, Southampton, Weston-super-Mare, Rugby (for 14 years) and finally Newton Abbot. Few M & S employees can have surpassed this travel record.

There is a limited amount of surviving information about staffing matters in the 1930s, just before the establishment of the Personnel Department in 1934. Most of it emanates from the Organisation Department, which was described in 1930 by Israel Sieff as 'the union joint, as it were, between the Departments here and the Stores'. It was endeavouring, he claimed, 'to sift all that is good for the business and reject all that is bad'.

There were references before 1934 to the Statistics Department and to the implications of government regulations for the business. Thus in 1932 it was laid down that no sales assistant under the age of 16 should be engaged in future either full-time or part-time and that all staff were entitled to proper holidays: 'Managers shall realise that it is not our policy to keep the staff at our stores working during their half holiday, for we believe that any alterations to displays can be done by staying an extra hour or two during one evening'.

Clearly staffing matters were being handled differently in different places, which explains why in 1930 two people were appointed who were 'to be regarded as Inspectors of Stores, whose duties were to visit stores and inspect them in the interests of the business . . . not as spies or policemen, but as representatives of Chiswell Street, sent out to help the Supervisors and Managers to merchandise the stores to the best advantage'. 'The introduction of another mind on these problems', Israel Sieff wrote after a conference of supervisors in February 1930, 'may bring fresh light on them and reveal them in such a way that it will be obvious both to the Supervisor and Manager that they are weaknesses that must be remedied. They may lift a manager out of a rut and give him a new focus on his work'.

On the 'welfare' side – though the term was not used until 1934 – there were references to stores where medical examinations of staff had been introduced (for porters as well as sales assistants) and many references to canteens, some of them bureaucratic in tone, like 'there appears to be some misapprehension regarding the definition of a "portion of bread and butter"', which meant 'three thin slices or as much as can be reasonably expected for 1d'. There were also many references to staff purchases. Members of staff were given a discount of 2d in the shilling, and were obviously regular customers.

Finally, there were rules relating to good management of the store, dealing with 'irregularities', like displays without price tags, misrepresentation of goods (always taken very seriously), the handling of mail, the reception of visitors, fire precautions, store security and, not least, cleanliness. A detailed report on one particular store states that the water used for washing lemonade glasses was not changed often enough. 'In future make certain that this is done at your store and that one drop of Milton is added to each pail of water.'

There are many signs of interest in staff members as individuals. For example, stores were reminded that birthdays were to be noted. So also were 'the names of any Managers or men in training who excel in any branch of sport, giving details of their accomplishments or clubs for whom they have played'. Soon store libraries were referred to, along with staff dances.

The coming of the Welfare Department in 1934 was more than the climax of existing policies. It represented a genuine breakthrough, fostering a sense of belonging among all M & S staff at work and at play. Many social activities of the 1930s are recalled by long-serving members of staff and by pensioners, including amateur dramatic societies, concerts, cricket matches and swimming galas, as well as memorable holiday outings and trips abroad. The Welfare Department arranged these. It also ensured a common staffing policy in all M & S stores, a policy which was to evolve through the years, but always according to the same principles.

The relationship between M & S and its staff did not end with retirement. One long-standing feature of M & S policy has been to invite back its pensioners to stores and head office regularly; and a *St Michael News* of 1982 included the memorable answer of one pensioner when asked what it was like to leave M & S after all these years. 'I replied', the pensioner said, 'that I really hadn't left, but was just getting paid a little less for doing nothing. I was still very much part of the M & S family, and was treated as such'.

Staff at a holiday camp at Dymchurch, Kent, in 1936.

Gentlemen, meet the new man. Marks & Spencer's promise to change him at any branch if he doesn't suit."

CARTOON COMMENT ON THE APPOINTMENT IN 1979 OF SIR DEREK (NOW LORD) RAYNER

AS AN ADVISER TO THE GOVERNMENT

FOLKLORE

o you
ve that
ry ever
peats
self,
ncer?"

From the very beginning of its history M & S had its folklore. Indeed, the folklore goes back even earlier to a reported (and undated) conversation between Michael Marks, Isaac Dewhirst, and Dewhirst's young assistant, Charlie Backhouse. Michael Marks is said to have been looking for work at Barran Clothiers, a well-known firm in Leeds, which by the 1880s was employing over 2,000 workers, many of them Jews. According to the folklore, one of the few English words Michael Marks knew was 'Barrans'.

The story goes that Dewhirst was so fascinated by the stranger from Poland that he asked him to his warehouse, and when he learned that he was looking for work and had no money, he offered to lend him £5. Michael asked (in what language is not certain) whether he could use the £5 to buy goods from the warehouse and, when he was told that he could, this first £5 was soon followed by others. It was a precept among Jews in Leeds, as elsewhere, that 'if you have poor and needy in your midst, do not let them become a charge on the Gentile community, look after them yourselves'. Through the help of Dewhirst, the gentile, however, Michael Marks never looked back. By the year 1888, when large numbers of Jewish immigrants to Leeds, who were working 12 hours a day in clothing sweatshops, went on an unsuccessful strike for better working conditions, Michael Marks had established himself as an independent retailer.

The story may have an element of truth in it. Yet, leaving on one side the key question of whether or not Michael Marks started in Leeds, what has hitherto been left out of the account is that in 1884 Dewhirst himself was only 21 years old. Far from being a well-established wholesaler with a secure business behind him, he had only just started his own business after a romantic journey around the world.

Given that reminiscence has always played such a big part in the continuing life of M & S, if only because so many people have worked in the business for long periods of time, often to be followed by their children, it is necessary to remember the old adage, 'success has a hundred fathers'. The folklore of success needs to be critically, if sympathetically, examined. Yet there is one reminiscence of success which rings very true. F.M. Smith, former Secretary of the company, recalled that when the London Penny Bazaar Company was bought from the Estermans, giving M & S a remarkable new foothold in London before the First World War, the Esterman brothers gave a dinner at the Trocadero restaurant (off Piccadilly Circus). There was a miniature castle standing in the centre of the table with a flag at the top inscribed with the one word 'Success'.

The folklore of M & S relates to the whole concern and not just to the individuals associated with it. The Manchester store, for example, once received a letter from Hong Kong addressed:
    Manager,
    Marks and Spencer (a large shop)
    Down Town, Manchester
    England.

A supervisor at Bristol, while staying at a hotel in Devon, heard a fellow guest telling a French tourist about places he should visit. One of them was 'the working man's paradise'. 'Where's that?' the Frenchman asked. 'M&S', was the reply. The term 'Marks & Sparks' has passed into the English language. It was included in the Supplement to the sixth edition of Eric Partridge's *Dictionary of Slang and Unconventional English*, published in 1967, where it was described as 'a neat rhyming jingle'. (Other new words or phrases introduced in this edition were 'gear', 'groovy', 'grotty' and 'with it'.)

In the Dutch daily newspaper *De Telegraaf* in January 1961 a writer claimed that M&S have 'done more for the people than Marx and Engels', a statement which has subsequently been repeated in many languages, including English, French and Swedish as well as Hebrew. So, too, has the term 'Marksist revolution'. Indeed, as early as 1938 the London Labour leader Lord Snell had written 'When I was young I read Herbert Spencer and Karl Marx ... Now I cannot estimate the debt I owe to Marks and Spencer'.

CHIC-FEED

"What a brilliant suggestion!—St. Michael, patron saint of marketing."

Alfred Lister, for many years the manager of the Derby Street warehouse, recalled being interviewed by Spencer in 1901 before he took up his first job – at the age of 13. 'He was loud of voice when he had occasion to chase us up a bit', Mr Lister remembered. And he remembered, too, how Spencer insisted on the boys unravelling the knots in all the string which had been used to tie up parcels and knocking the kinks out of nails so that they could be used again. At Christmas, however, there were bonuses. The largest he ever received was 9s 7d.

Elizabeth Harper of Manchester, born in 1888, told her daughter, Sarah Coogan, of how when she worked in Manchester M&S as a girl, Spencer would 'find time to travel to the girls' homes and back to the stores however long it took'. This was to make sure that they were allowed enough time to get home for lunch. He insisted that the girls needed 'a good meal to do the work properly'. 'Mr Marks', Sarah Coogan went on, 'did most of the buying at that time. He would go to the potteries and buy big baskets or skeps, not knowing the contents'.

Certainly Marks knew what he was selling. According to Mrs Hazel Logan, Marks often visited her mother and grandmother, who had once kept a penny stall in Leeds Market near his, when they subsequently moved to nearby Bingley. 'Mr Marks knocked at the door of their off-licence shop and showed them from his tray various items such as needles, toys and "fents", which are apparently small fabric cuts from the floor of local tailors'.

Harry Sacher tells a story of Michael Marks being told of pilfering at the first branch of M&S in London. 'Have they left the baskets?' Michael asked and, on being told that they had, he said, 'Then fill them up again.'

A story from the opening of the penny bazaar in the Cross Arcade (Leeds) in 1904 shows the excitement of nineteenth-century retailing. One of the girls on duty on the opening day is said to have estimated that the takings would not exceed £75, but Michael Marks contradicted her and told her they would reach £100. They were both wrong, for the takings had reached £175 by closing time (far more than the initial takings at Sunderland, the store with the earliest surviving records).

"We'll have the '57 Chateau St. Michael!"

There are many recorded memories of Marks, some of them collected from early M&S sales assistants by their relatives. Mrs S. Davies, born in 1892, had a sister 10 years older than herself – one of a family of 10 – who worked at the Birkenhead store and who recalled Michael as a very small man with a big heart, 'always humming to himself'. She remembered taking her tea to the store at Christmas 1900, when the store was so busy that her sister could not get back home:

> 'When I got to the stall Mr Marks (Michael Marks) came to me, took the basket off me and told me he would give it to her and told me to hurry home before it got too dark. There were no lights them days in the street, and I will always remember he bent down and took my hand and wished me a Merry Xmas. He must have asked my sister how many there were in the family and two weeks after Xmas a big hamper came to my Mother's house full of toys, most of them were broken or he could not sell. We were only kids but he made our day. No wonder they call him St Michael.'

"And to think we would never have met if you hadn't popped into Marks and Sparks for a pair of underpants"

That again is real folklore. And there are many stories of the attractions of Marks's stalls which were 'always the last to close on a Saturday night'. Indeed, Marks's very first stall in Leeds was described by a neighbouring tradesman, who worked a fruit stall in the market for 50 years, as a major attraction in a market where there were many competitive attractions, like 'a man called Sloman with hair dyed white on one side and black on the other who sold all sorts of ointments'. He would 'start up with a bird whistling', to get an audience, 'and after a bit one or two assistants would hand out his soap or ointment. Then there was the strong man who would start bending nails and selling some sort of lotion that if you took it would make you as strong as him'.

Walter Speer, warehouse foreman, on his return from military service in the First World War, married Rosa North, who worked at the Mile End (London) warehouse (at 9s a week). 'On August Bank Holiday, 1919', she reminisced in 1961, 'we were engaged. Until that time he used to buy whipped cream walnuts for the girls in the Warehouse, but from then on he very tactfully distributed them *via* me. Although it was a whirlwind courtship, we had been on very friendly terms. When Walter had visited the Warehouse on leave from France all the girls clubbed together and bought him a special fish and chip dinner and cigarettes as a special luxury. We got married on 13 December 1919 and I left in the following April. I was the youngest among the warehouse girls, but the most forward, I suppose, to have got married first. It was hard in those times to find time to get wed. Staff was short, and being Christmas we were very busy, working up to 9 o'clock every evening, 6 o'clock on Saturdays.... I had Friday, Saturday and the following week, but Walter had only Saturday, so we never had a honeymoon'.

A different example of a family involvement – this time, the creation of a dynasty – was started by Gladys Bowley, who began work at the age of 14 at the North End Road, Fulham branch. She worked her way up from sales assistant to manageress of another branch in 1910, and when she left there her place was taken by her sister Nellie Irene. Three of her other sisters worked for M & S too, and in 1968, when she was over 80 years old, her family was still represented in the business by her niece, Mrs Arnold.

Even when links of kinship are missing, friendships generated inside M & S often have a family quality about them. At Keighley six of the very first assistants remained close friends 40 years later, meeting regularly 'to talk about old times and the days when 19s was a very high wage for a young lady!' They held a special reunion to celebrate the fortieth anniversary of the opening of the store. And

CHRISTMAS 19 44 GREETINGS

1591-1944

M & S in wartime. Right: *The Marksman*, the Spitfire fighter financed by £5000 donated by the company in 1941. Right, below: M & S recruits at Greenhill Barracks, Woolwich, in July 1940. It had been hoped to form the recruits into an M & S Unit of the RAOC; in the event, they were dispersed to various RAOC units in the UK and overseas. Below: Clothing bearing the Utility Scheme label, as seen here, was exempt from purchase tax.

IN THE HOUR OF PERIL
MARKS AND SPENCER
LIMITED
EARNED THE GRATITUDE
OF THE BRITISH NATIONS
SUSTAINING THE VALOUR OF
THE ROYAL AIR FORCE
AND FORTIFYING THE CAUSE
OF FREEDOM
BY THE GIFT OF
SPITFIRE AIRCRAFT
They shall mount up with wings as eagles
Issued by the Ministry of Aircraft Production
1941

there is at least one M & S character who has made a point of trying to visit *every* store – Sam Worton, 'Cycling Sam' – who after five years reached journey's end at Michael House in Baker Street on Monday, 27 September 1955 as scheduled. In one week in June of that final year he had visited 39 stores in the London area as part of his final mopping-up operation. He met more than once a number of managers who had transferred from one store to another during the five-year period. One, N.F. Prince, he met three times – at West Hartlepool, Ipswich and Exeter.

One M & S sales assistant of the 1930s, Sylvia Crowe (later Mrs Franklin), kept a diary of her days in the M & S Lincoln store, which characteristically covers work and play. She started work on 5 September 1938, the youngest member of the staff, so that she had to leave early 'to conform to working hour rules', and it was only on 5 December, when she 'went out for a perm', that she felt 'grown up, like the others at work'. She had already joined the sports committee and had acquired a new winter uniform which 'closely resembled a schoolgirl's'.

The sports club was a 'great success', and its success went on to inspire a concert party as well. Work, however, could have its trials. 'There was a period', the diary notes read in February 1939, 'when we had to stay behind after the store was closed to inspect stock, searching for suspicious-looking parcels and envelopes'. The first Air Raid Precautions (ARP) lecture was in July of that year. When war broke out, 'our dear Mr Newland…was the first to volunteer' and he was killed during his initial training, 'which brought home to us the first horror of what was beginning'. Mrs. Franklin's diary notes end: 'We had something special in those years which gave us good training not only in salesmanship, store procedure and working together, but also finding a way to make the most of every minute of leisure time'.

A second reason why folklore in M & S counts is that retailing is the kind of business which generates jokes as well as anecdotes. The pace of the business is fast, and in the flow of words behind the scenes – sometimes, indeed, in front of them – there is ample scope for quick thinking. At 9 pm one Saturday night, E.A. Hubbard was patrolling the sales floor at the Holloway Road (London) store when he noticed a customer wandering round. He approached him, told him all the sales girls had gone home, and asked him what he was doing. 'Don't you know who I am?' the stranger asked. 'No', he replied. 'I am Simon Marks'. After Mr Hubbard had been subjected to some characteristically penetrating questions, they moved to the toy department, where Simon Marks tried out a yo-yo. 'They certainly need a lot of patience', Mr Hubbard said, to which Simon Marks responded, 'I have a great deal of that'.

Managers – and divisional superintendents – never followed one uniform pattern, but they often left a deep impression. They had to be quickwitted when occasion demanded it, as well as meticulous. There are many stories illustrating this. Thus, one day Vic Simons, manager of the Worthing store, thought that he saw a lady shoplifting. 'Just a moment, madam, I want to search your shopping bag'. But when he searched her bag he found that nothing was stolen. 'As I thought, madam', he said without hesitation, 'My sales assistant has overcharged you'. And he offered the customer a shilling, saying, 'Please accept this refund together with my most sincere apologies'.

Another manager, who invented a push-button buzzer service, was able to call certain members of his staff by pressing different coloured buttons. One day, when he was ill, the superintendent visited the store and, left alone in the Manager's office, decided to put the push-button service to the test. He found that the staff responded well until he pushed the last button which was a small red one. For about three minutes nothing happened. Then the door opened and in walked the barman from the public house next door with two flagons of beer, neatly wrapped in brown paper.

There are many anecdotes about 'welfare', including a revealing story of Lord Marks. A member of staff, laden with bundles of towels for the washrooms, was about to step into a lift when he saw Lord Marks and scurried away. 'Come in, you won't catch anything', said the Chairman. As the staff member left the lift at the fifth floor, Lord Marks called after him, 'Even if you do catch anything, we'll look after you!'

By May 1940, 550 out of 2,000 male employees were in the armed forces, and by the end of the war the figure had risen to over 1,500. 'We have been requested by the War Office to form a unit of the RAOC comprised of 225 employees of M & S', J. Edward Sieff wrote to members of staff eligible for military service in June 1940, and a month later 201 M & S recruits, including 10 managers, were on parade at Greenhill Barracks, Woolwich. After a six-week training period under 'a bunch of hardened regular drill sergeants', they were posted not to an M & S unit *en bloc*, but to different scattered units.

Thereafter, they usually kept in close touch with the stores or offices from which they had been recruited or with Neil Furse at head office, receiving the *Staff Bulletin* and sending in Christmas cards each year from all over the world. Of the store managers who were recruited then or at other times, over half were commissioned, as were more than a third of the head-office staff from Baker Street. Eighty-nine men were killed in action and 59 became prisoners of war; 77 were awarded decorations and distinctions.

Norman Laski was one of the directors whose expertise was used fully. For nearly six years he served as a Lieutenant-Colonel at an RAOC depot, where as part of his duties he would meet Michael Sieff, working at the War Office, and J.A. Grant, manager at Woolwich. Laski recalled after the war how interesting it had been to watch vast quantities of goods for the forces arriving from M & S peacetime suppliers, 'particularly the unmistakably familiar large bales of goods from Messrs Corah'.

M & S, in fact, made a remarkable contribution to the RAF during the Second World War, providing £5,000 to the national Spitfire fighter fund. The M & S Spitfire, named *The Marksman*, has itself passed into legend. Its most spectacular success was the shooting down in one afternoon of three enemy fighters. This and other exploits won the DFM for the pilot, Sergeant (later Squadron Leader, DFC) Rigler, who is alive and well in 1984.

In 1938 an engineer called R.A. Salaman was appointed to organise air-raid precautions. His contract was for six months: he remained with M & S until 1963. On his first morning at M & S he was given a desk and a secretary and asked to prepare recommendations for a meeting of directors that afternoon. He had not yet gathered his thoughts and in consequence produced a short report, 'which',

Many M & S stores were damaged or destroyed in bombing raids by the Luftwaffe in the Second World War. Left: Canterbury store, the morning after. Bottom, left: Temporary premises were used after the Coventry store was destroyed during the night of 14 November 1940. Bottom, right: A sign directing customers to temporary premises after bombs had destroyed the store in The Moor, Sheffield.

REMAINS OF CASH "FLOAT" BRISTOL STORE

Destroyed by Enemy Action Oct 1940.

MARKS & SPENCER L^{TD}
NEW PREMISES
LANSDOWNE CINEMA BUILDINGS
LONDON ROAD.

he added 45 years later, 'was perhaps just as well, for I soon discovered that Simon hated long ones'.

Many stores suffered from damage caused by enemy air attack, some severely. Birmingham, for example, became 'a smouldering ruin'; Clacton was 'burnt out'; Exeter 'simply collapsed' when a huge bomb fell on the furniture store opposite. At one Midlands store 24 incendiary bombs were smothered in a night. And there were M & S staff members who were killed or injured or rendered homeless. One of the most moving notes was from W. Stapleton, a firewatcher at Plymouth. 'At 11 pm I heard that my wife and children were killed, but I could do nothing about it so I carried on with the work at M & S . . . When dawn broke, we celebrated our victory in saving the premises by hoisting the Union Jack'.

After a raid, a detailed report was sent in at once to Salaman in the ARP Department in Baker Street. Boston reported that after an incendiary bomb had fallen on the store six dozen overalls and one hundredweight (50 kg) of lemonade powder had been damaged. Coventry described how the public – 'particularly children who were homeless' – had been helped by staff from the Leamington store. Salaman himself recalled M & S staff being given a cup of tea at Woolworth's in a town where the M & S store had been gutted by fire 'while some of our own stock, sodden with water, was being carried dripping across their undamaged sales floor up to the stockroom where it was to be kept for us'.

Salaman issued an *ARP Manual*, which stressed the need for precautions to be simple and the arrangements 'capable of quick change to meet changes in the enemies' method of attack'. It included a list of basic store records to be left in a metal document box: they included cash-books, branch stock ledgers, sundries ledgers, invoices not passed, goods and receipts lists, coupon and points record books. Far more of this documentary material, however, was to be destroyed in 'Operation Simplification' (see Chapter 7) than in 'Operation Hitler'.

Not all M & S folklore surrounds M & S personnel. Some of it concerns suppliers. One of the best early stories, told by a one-time associate of Michael Marks, relates to an unnamed supplier of 60 years ago who, in order to obtain a large contract from M & S, put a trial quantity into Kilburn store and then arranged that his entire family should visit the store quickly to buy up the stock.

M & S's first royal guest was Queen Mary, who visited Marble Arch store in 1932.

A supplier of a different kind, W. Hilton Farrar, who designed music covers (including *Hymns that Will Live for Ever*) and painting books for M & S before 1914, got in touch with M & S in 1956. He was, he said, 65 years old and had 'albums full of designs and prints of books which I am proud to say I sold in thousands. I would very much like a chance to work for the firm I served many years ago'. When Stuart Lisbona of M & S looked at the album, he discovered that a number of drawings were dated 1896 when, according to Hilton Farrar's reckoning, he would have been only five years old. He was, in fact, 86.

Visitors to M & S stores have their place in the history, too – beginning in 1932 with the first royal visitor, Queen Mary, who is said to have bought 6 handbags, 3 books (a Shakespeare and two Bibles at 1s 6d each), a rug (at 2s 11d), a baby doll (at 5s), a 21-piece tea set (at 6s) and a willow-pattern teapot (at 1s) at the Oxford Street store. The Queen is said to have told Simon Marks that 'it was the most successful shopping she had ever done'. When she left the store, a crowd of people rushed to buy duplicate items. The Queen had also examined the Easter cards, and 'all the cards the Queen touched were bought within a quarter of an hour', an assistant told the *Evening Standard* reporter.

Later royal visitors have included the future Edward VIII when he was Prince of Wales, the present Prince of Wales, Princess Margaret, and Queen Elizabeth II, who visited Redditch in 1983. Among politicians who have visited M & S stores it is perhaps Aneurin Bevan (a close friend of Israel Sieff's) and Mrs Thatcher who have stood out. In particular, Mrs Thatcher's walkabout visit to the Marble Arch 'flagship store' in April 1983 produced a crop of stories as well as a battery of newspaper headlines and photographs. Complaining that the crowd was so big that she could not do any shopping, she nevertheless examined with interest a £75 pin-striped suit which she said would be 'just right' for her husband Denis. (The suit was duly delivered to 10 Downing Street soon afterwards.)

Among foreign visitors Eleanor Roosevelt, widow of the former President of the United States, was singled out by the manager of the Pantheon. She arrived at one day's notice in April 1948, accompanied by Lady Reading, and was received by Norman Laski, Mrs Solomon and Marcus Sieff. She visited a training class, studied the canteen menus, and tasted some M & S ice cream.

Buildings as well as people have their folklore, not least the Marble Arch store. If the Pantheon was full of ghosts as well as of customers, Marble Arch was one of the seven twentieth-century wonders of the world for customers from all over the globe, including Arab states. At Christmas 1983 weekly takings were well over the £2 million mark. At an earlier Christmas, due to an unprecedented volume of business, bundles of sales assistants' uniforms were by accident placed on display and were sold as dresses within half an hour.

Old buildings have their romance as well as the new. In Newcastle, Grainger Market stall remains, and writing on its seventieth birthday, Gladys Graham, then manager, said that she would never work anywhere else. 'There is the interest of the other stalls and of getting to know the stallholders for a start. Then one girl has to go out and get the free tea, another has the washing up to do, and the floor in front of the store has to be mopped each morning – the staff take turns with these extra duties. In the winter, of course, it can blow very cold and the girls have special foam-backed jackets and woollen stockings as part of their staff uniform'. Just across the way from the stall is a butcher's and poultry business that belonged to William Colman, and which still trades under that name. Colman's wife was the first manageress of the Grainger Market penny bazaar.

If Grainger Market represents M & S antiquities, during the building of M & S stores many other local antiquities have been unearthed. At Winchester, for example, there is a plaque on the store which reads 'King John gave the property on this site about 1212 to his tailor, who in return was to supply yearly a fine coat'. Not surprisingly, when Bovis extended the store during the 1970s, the workers on the site were asked to watch out for archaeological finds.

At Bath a ewer containing a skull was dug up; at Worcester second-century pots and bowls were discovered; at Doncaster a Roman legionary shield; at Norwich glazed earthenware pottery of the seventeenth and eighteenth centuries was found; and at King's Lynn finds included a gold dish, bronze buttons, belt fastenings and pins of the thirteenth, fourteenth and fifteenth centuries, silver Edward I coins and a wine pitcher.

Top: The Queen in conversation with sales staff during her visit to Redditch store in 1983. Middle: Margaret Thatcher visited the Marble Arch store in April 1983. Bottom: Suits bought for Denis Thatcher being delivered to 10 Downing Street, after the Prime Minister had admired one of the pin-striped range.

Ten years later, far away in Perth (Tayside), when a new M & S property was acquired, a major excavation was carried out in 1975 which Leslie Alcock, Professor of Archaeology at Glasgow, called an 'outstanding success'. Whole classes of archaeological materials were discovered which had not been found elsewhere in Scotland, according to Nicholas Bagden, the excavation director. At Aberdeen the historic Wallace Tower, constructed around 1600, was removed in 1965 when the new M & S store was opened, and reconstructed stone by stone on a new site. In Glasgow a tablet on the Argyll Street store reads: 'Robert Burns lodged here (in 1788), when this building was the Black Bull Inn'.

In York a sixteenth-century mantelpiece found in a panelled room in premises acquired for store extension in 1925 was handed over to the Company of Merchant Venturers, whose arms it bore. 'The spontaneity of the action', the *Yorkshire Herald* remarked, 'was all the more magnanimous because of the fact that the firm is composed of London men, and not of York citizens!' In London itself the Pantheon had always been recognised as one of the capital's most interesting historic sites. Designed by James Wyatt, the original Pantheon had been opened as a centre for masquerades and concerts in 1772 (with a great rotunda and four Nollekens statues of Britannia, Liberty, the King and the Queen), and in 1789 it had been converted into an opera house. After serving later as a theatre, it was rebuilt in 1833 and used as a bazaar. From 1867 to 1937 W. & A. Gilbey, the wine merchants, turned it into an office and showroom.

Brand-new stores can have their folklore also. When Kingston opened in 1967, it became the longest M & S store: at 125 metres (401 feet) it beat Reading, formerly the longest, by over 18 metres (60 feet). 'When are you going to install a monorail?' a pensioner is said to have asked. Belfast, opened in 1967 – and, despite all the troubles in Northern Ireland, one of M & S's most successful stores – has another unusual record. The foundations had to be laid 5 metres (17 feet) lower than was usual in the city, and 450 concrete piles, 15 to 21 metres (50 to 70 feet) long, were sunk into the sludge. There were said to have been more people there – 120,000, many of them from across the border – on opening day than at the opening day of any other store.

The tea services were often treasured through the years. In 1965 Gladys Huntley of Pontypridd reported having kept one for 31 years. She had given it as a wedding present to her sister, who allowed no one, except herself and Gladys, ever to wash it up. Mrs Beck of Plymouth confessed that the remaining balance of her set was one bread-and-butter plate, six tea plates and five saucers. 'The cups unfortunately slipped through my fingers when I was much younger and, now that I am a pensioner, I expect the plates and saucers will follow suit'. Mrs Adams of Heald Green, Cheshire, had been even less lucky. 'I have a pot fruit set, six small and one large dish, purchased in 1936 at the old Market Street store, priced 1s 11d old money. It was called the Orange Grove. I originally had the tea set, of which now I only have a bread-and-butter plate'. The first set, however, was 'in constant use'. When in 1980 pensioners reported what old M & S wares they still possessed, Mrs E. Minlin said that she still had a complete tea set of St Michael bone china, polka-dot design.

As time has passed by, M & S watches have figured prominently also in domestic archaeology. One pensioner, W. G. Sadler, reported in 1980 what he called 'a wrist watch with a story':

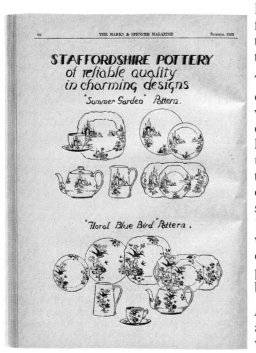

Bought for me by my wife from Brixton store in 1936/7, price 4s 6d plus 6d for strap, it served time with me through many hard knocks. Square-bashing, duties as gunner/armourer and even a spot of bomb disposal it took as a mere hand's turn. Later, on OCTU battle-drills and courses, it journeyed several times into unexpected culverts and flooded drains, twice being rushed despairingly to a cleaners, and one time falling down an 80-foot cliff; but came through it all with truly beating heart. It was worn all day, every day, accompanying me to India and into Burma, when I used cloth straps (until I ran out of 'em). It took part in 'Combined Ops' and inadvertent sea bathing in a wet landing, pickled in salt, I guess, until the monsoons washed it, but 'time' went on although I got hospitalised.

Eventually I got back to this country in October 1945 with dear old faithful still ticking steadily. Then I made a sad, fatal mistake. I thought to reward my old friend with a fine, new, clean strap – and half the back of old-timer was rusted too and came away with the old strap! It ticked for a few more seconds, then shuddered to a deathly silence and I almost shed tears.

Five bob's worth! I don't think my £50 presentation one would give that sort of service.

Turning to textiles, a jumper was sent to Marcus Sieff in 1980 'given to my eldest brother, secondhand, before or during the last World War'. 'It has been in almost daily use since then', Mr Davies, a doctor, wrote, 'a tremendous tribute to the quality of your goods'. (Mr Davies was sent two replacements from the current range with a request for a further report after another 40 to 45 years on how they had worn.) One M & S dress was worn (not every day) by three generations.

Only a few letters from customers have passed into folklore, like the reply to a letter of 1968 asking why chickens' claws were never supplied with chicken giblets, though they were necessary for gravy. The reply read, 'It is suggested that the only time claws are supplied with a chicken would be when purchasing from a butcher undressed'. That was not the end of the affair since the complainant insisted that claws were an essential part of good gravy-making. She added that she was receiving pension money from the Prudential, 'who financed M & S', and was consulting her lawyer 'to investigate the affairs of M & S in order to protect my financial interests there and to uphold the rights of the Crown'.

Another letter of 1976 complained of the contents of a bottle of Côtes-du-Rhône, an 'honest, but "bad-tempered" wine', scarcely calculated to uplift. 'No doubt', the letter-writer went on – and he insisted that he was not complaining – 'it was (of the kind) being served with the last dinner in the main saloon of the Titanic'. The M & S response was appropriate. 'We are naturally sorry that this particular wine did not suit you although, in defence, it is one of our more popular wines. Rather than subject you to the trauma of tasting another bottle of the same, we have enclosed with this letter a bottle of our champagne'.

Perhaps the best of all the M & S anecdotes needs no picture, and it comes appropriately enough from Oxford. An elderly lady complained about M & S merchandise: 'Since St Michael took over your firm I have been unable to find anything that fits me'.

Above: A display of 5 shilling and half-crown watches in an M & S window in the 1930s. Not all underwent such tribulations as those reported by Mr Sadler (*see story at left*).

"Funny how it goes—he started with a little stall alongside Lord Marks."

AN EARLY TILL AND (INSET) A NOTE ON THE OPENING OF MICHAEL MARKS'S ACCOUNT WITH THE MIDLAND BANK IN 1897

PERFORMANCE

Leaving on one side all the folklore, the greatest achievement of M&S is not that it has grown into a huge concern with an international reputation, but that while it has grown it has achieved what two American historians of business, T.J. Peters and R.H. Waterman, have called 'corporate excellence'.

In their study *In Search of Excellence* (1982), which covered 12 American businesses, they identified eight attributes associated with their key concept: 'a bias for action, for getting on with it'; 'closeness to the consumer'; 'autonomy and entrepreneurship' in the interests of 'creative innovation'; 'productivity through people', which involves 'respect for the individual'; a 'value-driven' philosophy of the enterprise; 'sticking to the knitting' ('never acquiring a business you don't know how to run'); 'simple form, with lean staff'; and 'simultaneous loose-tight properties'. The last of these, they argued, involves a balance between centralisation and decentralisation – 'centralist round the core values', 'decentralist in pushing autonomy down to the shop floor or product development team'.

There is no attribute in this very American list which cannot be treated as an M&S label, although the language at Baker Street is very different. And while lip service would be paid to several of the attributes by any business organisation in any part of the world – almost everybody agrees that 'people are our most important asset' – M&S has never been interested in lip service. Before the deaths of Michael Marks and Tom Spencer, performance was measured very precisely – by results, by 'getting on with it' – but already by 1926, before the public company was formed, emphasis was being placed both on 'creative innovation' and on 'value-driven philosophy'. 'Sticking to the knitting' and 'simple form' were always either taken for granted or were proclaimed afresh with evangelistic fervour, as in 'Operation Simplification'.

The first Marks and Spencer performance record was a record of the profits Michael Marks and Tom Spencer shared and of the capital they left in the between market stalls and bazaar stores in general shopping areas. When in 1907 and costs of individual stores – with particular attention being paid to profit margins – and it is from these data that tables of turnover and average turnover per store have been prepared. One early table (*see right*) summarised the results down to 1915.

Within the overall picture, profits were compared between particular stores and between market stalls and bazaar stores in general shopping areas. When in 1907 15 out of 49 M&S branches were in market halls and 34 were in shops, the average turnover of a market hall bazaar was £1,765, while the average turnover of a shop bazaar was £4,180. Yet the profit differences were less substantial. The net profit of a market bazaar was £215 a year and of a shop £375. By 1914, when there were 143 branches, only 10 were in market halls, and the acquisition of the Esterman stores had led to a very careful evaluation of particular business properties. Rents, of course, were a factor also: they varied considerably. The kind of profit comparisons which were made of a number of market halls and shops are set out in the tables overleaf.

Below: Annual turnover of the company and average turnover per store for the years 1906-15.

YEAR	NO. OF STORES	TURNOVER £	AVERAGE TURNOVER PER STORE £
1906	49	151,000	3,100
1907	49	169,000	3,400
1908	53	177,000	3,300
1909	57	200,000	3,500
1910	67	217,000	3,200
1911	89	268,000	3,000
1912	107	317,000	3,400
1913	114	355,000	3,100
1914	143	393,000	2,700
1915	145	408,000	2,800

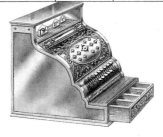

MARKS &SPENCER — MARKETS

Comparative profitability of selected market stall[s and] shops, 1906-14. The figures represent profits as a percentage of turnover.

MARKETS	1906	1907	1908	1909	1910	1911	1912	1913	1914
ASHTON	12.8	14.4	14.1	15.5	16.0	14.3	15.3	15.6	19.3
BOLTON	12.8	14.4	14.3	15.5	16.0	14.3	13.5	12.5	18.3
BIRKENHEAD	15.7	15.7	14.6	15.4	15.7	16.4	14.1	7.5	19.1
BIRMINGHAM	11.8	12.9	11.1	10.3	9.5	6.7	6.7	9.3	11.4
CARDIFF	13.3	14.0	13.9	14.7	14.0	12.3	10.4	13.7	12.6
HUDDERSFIELD	9.4	11.9	10.4	11.8	12.1	12.0	12.3	16.0	17.7
NEWCASTLE	14.6	14.7	14.7	17.6	17.5	18.5	18.1	12.5	19.1
STALYBRIDGE	16.0	16.9	15.4	15.8	15.3	14.9	14.2	13.0	16.4
SHEFFIELD	15.4	16.4	14.5	16.2	15.2	14.6	13.6	10.0	17.6
WAKEFIELD	10.6	10.9	9.2	10.9	10.4	10.1	8.4		14.6

SHOPS

SHOPS	1906	1907	1908	1909	1910	1911	1912	1913	1914
BIRMINGHAM	2.9	7.2	3.4	8.8	10.2	10.0	11.2	10.5	14.6
BLACKPOOL	8.7	9.0	7.5	11.2	12.2	12.7	12.7	12.2	15.1
BRISTOL	11.6	12.6	11.1	11.1	13.6	13.1	11.3	10.0	13.3
BRIXTON	9.2	8.2	10.0	13.2	13.1	12.0	13.4	14.4	15.7
CHELTENHAM	12.5	12.7	3.7	7.1	7.3	7.3	9.9	8.5	13.0
DOUGLAS	12.6	11.9	12.4	15.6	15.7	15.3	15.5	14.6	18.7
GRIMSBY	11.9	12.5	11.5	14.3	13.6	13.1	12.9	12.5	17.2
HULL	12.8	15.3	14.7	17.3	17.4	15.4	14.8	14.8	19.5
HARROGATE	8.3	7.2	8.9	14.1	15.8	15.9	15.8	15.0	20.0
ISLINGTON	3.0	0.2	–	–	3.3	3.7	6.5	7.0	8.5
LEEDS	2.7	3.1	4.2	2.0	19.3	0.5	2.7	7.2	8.6
LEICESTER	5.7	6.0	5.9	8.8	10.0	7.0	2.9	4.1	9.6
LIVERPOOL	12.5	12.0	12.8	14.8	14.9	14.2	13.7	13.0	16.5
MIDDLESBROUGH	8.5	9.4	8.7	11.5	13.5	12.4	11.9	11.8	17.1
READING	8.4	7.8	8.5	11.2	14.4	16.1	16.4	16.1	19.8
SOUTHPORT	6.9	9.6	10.2	12.4	12.1	5.1	8.7	11.8	16.2
SUNDERLAND	13.3	13.4	13.1	16.8	16.7	15.5	14.9	13.8	18.4
SOUTH SHIELDS	12.7	11.6	4.8	10.7	10.9	11.5	11.5	11.1	16.3
SOUTHWARK	3.6	4.7	3.8	6.8	7.7	8.5	6.6	7.6	12.5
STOCKTON	12.5	12.9	5.6	9.2	9.6	10.8	10.1	8.5	13.4

For each individual store there are detailed records of costs and profits between 1906 and 1910. For comparisons between three Yorkshire bazaars in 1906 see the upper table in the column (*right*).

Unfortunately, while total turnover is recorded – and it rose from £151,000 in 1906 to £850,573 in the last year of the old company – there are no continuous records of individual stores which reach beyond the First World War to the year of the formation of the new company in 1926. Nor do the published records after 1926 give details of turnover in particular lines, although they do give composite figures of 'stock in trade' and include occasional odd items like 'plate-glass renewal fund', £100 (1927) and £200 (1928). Total turnover figures exist for all these years, although 'turnover' is not mentioned as such in the published accounts until 1960, when a 10-yearly progress record was conveniently set out for the first time. There are also figures before and after 1926 on the costs of leasing (or buying) properties and of necessary maintenance and improvement.

There are figures on the employment of and return on capital from 1927, when the return was 7.6%. By 1939 it had risen to 19% (the peak figure was 20.4% at the height of the Depression in 1933). Meanwhile, profits and dividends rose from £74,939 and 7% in 1927 to £1,781,958 and 42.5% in 1939.

Turning to more recent history, it is interesting to compare the position in 1964, when Simon Marks died, with the position in 1983/4. Turnover in 1964 was £201,496,000, and in 1983/4 it was £2,854,500,000. Profits before tax in 1964 were £25 million; and in 1983/4 were £279.3 million, more in money terms than the turnover of 1964.

In 1983/4 £5.8 million was allotted to staff profit sharing. During that year 2,500 new jobs were created. Performance figures not included in the Chairman's statement included the fact that St Michael accounted for over 15% of the United Kingdom market in clothing (the share was over 30% in the case of some items), and that over 10% of the United Kingdom consumption of chickens, cakes, and cream came from M & S sales.

It would be interesting to have comparative figures of the share of turnover in textiles and food in early periods in the history of M & S. There is a series in existence, however, from 1933 to 1983, as is shown in the table (*right, below*).

Perhaps a more revealing comparison of performance is that between M & S in 1972/3, just after Lord (Marcus) Sieff took over as Chairman, and 1983/4. It is best stated in tabular form (*see upper table, page 117*).

Such extraordinary growth took place in one of the most trying decades in British economic history. Yet it was growth based on growth. J. Edward Sieff had been able to claim a record year in 1971/2, and to announce an annual dividend of 31¼%. He had also been able to announce the addition of 250,000 square feet of selling space and the fact that exports had doubled since the devaluation of the pound in 1967. Indeed, he produced his own 10-year statement, covering the years 1963 to 1972 (*see lower table on page 116*), which it is interesting to compare with the growth patterns from 1972/3 to 1983/4.

The first 10-year table, produced in 1960, had covered the shift from austerity to 'affluence' and the beginnings of the remarkable transformation of the business against the background of the developing society. They had been years when

	LEEDS ARCADE	KEIGHLEY	YORK
RENT	£650 0s 0d	£40 0s 0d	£1571 0s 0d
LIGHTING	£219 11s 9d	£28 12s 4d	£93 10s 0d
WAGES	£632 10s 3d	£87 19s 9d	£178 16s 0d
SUNDRIES	£16 3s 6d	£2 4s 10d	£9 6s 9d
RATES AND WATER	£242 1s 0d	£11 15s 0d	£58 9s 06d
COMMISSION	£108 14s 11d	£11 15s 10d	£45 6s 3d
PAPER AND BAGS	£65 5s 3d	£7 3s 1d	£27 3s 8d
CARRIAGE	£137 0s 8d	£16 1s 6d	£83 15s 1d
TRAVELLING	£43 10s 2d	£4 15s 5d	£18 2s 5d
DEPRECIATION	–	–	£67 14s 5d
WASTE	£142 10s 6d	£16 9s 11d	£14 8s 9d
DEFICIENCY	£385 12s 3d	£54 2s 5d	£63 9s 5d
HEAD OFFICE EXPENSES	£174 0s 10d	£19 1s 7d	£72 9s 10d
TOTAL TAKINGS	£8701 18s 0d	£953 16s 9d	£3624 15s 6d

Above: Comparison of performance of three Yorkshire bazaars in 1906.

Below: Percentages of turnover accounted for by textiles (left-hand figures) and food (right-hand figures), 1933-83.

Year	Textiles	Food
1933	89	11
1938	80	20
1943	68	32
1948	69	31
1953	80	20
1958	85	15
1963	78	22
1968	72	28
1973	72	28
1978	69	31
1983	64	36

YEAR ENDED 31 MARCH	1951	1952	1953	1954	1955	1956	1957	1958	1959	1960
TURNOVER	65,836	75,856	86,931	94,806	108,375	119,400	125,012	130,429	134,449	148,023
PROFIT BEFORE TAXATION	6,082	4,996	6,741	7,867	9,268	10,130	12,806	14,143	15,059	17,806
NET PROFIT AFTER TAXATION	2,557	2,306	2,466	3,017	4,468	4,955	5,606	6,193	7,709	9,081
NET DIVIDENDS TO SHAREHOLDERS	937	1,005	1,282	1,675	2,365	2,660	3,181	3,441	4,132	5,384

Above: The first 10-year-performance table, produced in 1960. Below: J. Edward Sieff's 10-year statement for 1963-72. The figures in both tables represent £000s.

YEAR ENDED 31 MARCH	1963	1964	1965	1966	1967	1968	1969	1970	1971	1972
TURNOVER	184,878	201,494	219,791	238,015	255,770	282,306	317,336	360,935	416,685	463,022
PROFIT BEFORE TAXATION	22,305	24,920	27,506	29,618	30,659	33,871	38,123	43,705	50,115	53,766
NET PROFIT AFTER TAXATION	10,955	12,070	12,706	18,268	18,959	20,121	21,773	24,955	31,215	34,416
NET DIVIDENDS TO SHAREHOLDERS	7,745	8,567	9,258	9,928	9,950	10,266	10,609	11,928	13,904	15,528

Simon Marks, in the words of his *Financial Times* obituary in 1964, stood out as 'the genius of the retail trade'. 'He was a maker of huge profits', the obituary went on, 'but placed money-making well down on his list of priorities'. It is for this reason that the account of 'performance' set out briefly in this chapter must be supported by an account of the philosophy of the M & S business in the next. Yet performance at this crucial stage had been striking, as is shown in the table (*opposite page, above*).

Two further features of performance require fuller attention, however: foreign business and exports. This history is concerned primarily with the United Kingdom, 'a nation of customers'. Yet M & S was interested in exports during the Second World War (an M & S Export Corporation was set up in 1940), and by 1955 was exporting goods to the value of £703,000. The first time the million-pound mark was reached was 1963 (£1,506,000); and between 1974 and 1977 exports trebled from £13.6 million to £40.4 million. It was in 1977 that M & S won the Queen's Award for Export Achievement.

It was because M & S was already involved in the export of St Michael goods to Canada that it decided to go into direct selling there and opened its first Canadian store in 1972 at Brampton, 30 miles from Toronto. Two years later M & S had 17 stores scattered across the country and, by 1977, 69.

The first Paris store, opened in 1975, and later stores in France and in Belgium, were opened for the same reason, although in this case the entry of Britain into the European Community was an additional factor.

St Michael merchandise is exported to 30 countries. Much of it is sold in locally owned shops, called St Michael stores, and selling only M & S goods. These can be found around the world – in, for instance, Gibraltar, Bermuda, Bahamas, Cyprus, and Jersey. St Michael merchandise can also be seen in many other countries, including Singapore, Malaysia, Japan, Panama, and South Africa. In 1983 one of the most remarkable export achievements was to sell to Hong Kong 1,000 dozen M & S long-sleeved shirts made in the United Kingdom. And in the same year £400,000-worth of M & S goods were exported to Iceland, whose population is just over 200,000.

	1972/3	1983/4
AVERAGE WEEKLY NUMBER OF EMPLOYEES	26,593	33,923
		1,254
		3,866
NUMBER OF STORES	248	262
		9
		213
TOTAL SALES AREA (000 SQ FT)	5,059	6,971
		262
		2,220
TOTAL TURNOVER EXCLUDING SALES TAXES (£M)	496	2,854
SALES PER EMPLOYEE (£)	18,651	73,099
UK STORE SALES EXCLUDING SALES TAXES (£M)	485	2,597
UK STORE SALES PER SQUARE FOOT (£)	96	372
UK PROFIT BEFORE TAX (£M)	70	265
UK PROFIT PER SQUARE FOOT (£)	14	38

Above: Comparison of performance, 1972/3 and 1983/4.

LOCATION	OPENING DATE
PARIS: BOULEVARD HAUSSMANN	1975
BRUSSELS	1975
LYON	1975
PARIS: ROSNY 2	1977
DUBLIN	1979
REIMS	1980
STRASBOURG	1981
LILLE	1982
ANTWERP	1983

COVER OF *SPARKS*, THE M & S HOUSE MAGAZINE, FOR SUMMER 1937

PHILOSOPHY

Left: An article on economic prospects by Israel Sieff, which was published in *Sparks* in the summer of 1937.

When Israel Sieff recalled the 1920s some 50 years later in 1970, it was not so much 'the development of M & S as a trading organisation' which made him rejoice, but 'its growth and maturing as a function of society'. Performance, therefore, had to be measured in something more than statistics.

In one of the best-written articles in *Sparks*, Cyril G. Naylor described his 'first store' in the 1930s. After an unforgettable first week, which began in a cellar below stairs into which poured 'a ceaseless avalanche' of richly varied merchandise, he ended on the Saturday night, 'cleansed and in my best suit', on a 'glamorous and crowded' sales floor, where it was later announced that the previous highest sale had been beaten, and then and there, 'standing amid the debris of paper bags and scattered humbugs, pale and voiceless, I knew for the first time a triumph without flaw'.

Another fascinating article by the editor of *Sparks*, which appeared in the very first number in the spring of 1934, was called 'Fugitives in a Chain Store'. It also began with 'the first day in the store…the very longest in our lives and the most bewildering'. It dealt with the whole process of promotion from first assistant to store manager, included a visit to head office, and ended with the return of an enthusiastic manager to his store. 'There's no fun like congenial work', the editor concluded. 'It grows on you and gets you like fever. What a scope there is for originality and experimenting. Finally, who wouldn't be a fugitive in our chain of stores?'

Both articles caught the spirit of successful retailing during the inter-war years, but Naylor added an extra note which he modestly called a digression. His store was a community as well as a place where goods were bought in and sold. On the Saturday, 'as night enfolded the grim industrial town, the store, with its light and warmth, beckoned the tired folk, free at last from loom and mill, inviting them to dally and stare at leisure. And here was treasure within the reach of the most modest purse'. And remembering how things had already changed by the late 1940s, he went on: 'That all levels of class and income seek their needs in our Stores is a commonplace now, but in those days when the Lancashire lass doffed her clogs and shawl it was to M & S she came to widen her horizons with the brighter clothes and adornment she deserved'.

With such history, what need is there of philosophy? Long before the outbreak of the Second World War, M & S was a successful business with a social reputation. Its experiences threw new light on the old Jewish precept, 'a good name is better than good oil', for M & S acquired the best of names while at the same time providing the best of oils.

Yet at least since the early days of Simon Marks and Israel Sieff M & S, as this book has insisted, has had a conscious philosophy. The principles set out in the first chapter have remained firm however much the patterns of social life have changed. The art and science of retailing have lain in knowing how to apply them. And they are principles which have been widely proclaimed, for M & S

Lord (Marcus) Sieff, son of Israel Sieff and grandson of Michael Marks, is President of M & S. He was Chairman from 1972 until July 1984.

chairmen, directors and managers have never hesitated to export their message as well as their goods. For them the fact that the 'outside world' often looks like a clumsy, inefficient and divided world is a challenge, not a reason for ignoring it.

To be confident and optimistic is not to be unselfcritical, and the present Lord Sieff has recently quoted another old Jewish precept, which comes from a commentary on the Old Testament: 'without knowledge there is no understanding and without understanding there is no knowledge'. Any modern business which lacked knowledge, including technical knowledge, would never be a success. The laboratory, where things could be tested and processes unravelled, became an indispensable part of the business, therefore, a means to control and to maintain consistency. Yet understanding, Lord Sieff would insist, rests not just on achieving performance but on fostering attitudes. Testing does not stop in the laboratory. When directors visit stores to judge for themselves, they are testing. And when the newest sales assistant is dealing with her first customers, the advice the staff manageress gives her is directly concerned with attitudes.

It is because knowledge and understanding are thought to be necessary and mutually dependent qualities that spokesmen of M & S have consistently argued that the M & S philosophy is strictly relevant not only to the interests of the company, but to the interests of the country.

In his first speech to the House of Lords the present Lord Sieff dealt with the importance of knowledge and pointed to the strategic role of new industries based on a modern technology, for which there will be a growing market. He spoke with approval of the ways in which technology is making possible the creation of wholly novel industries, which will use less energy and which will be of key importance to the world economy in the next century. Such technical innovation presented an opportunity and a challenge to which British industry must respond.

In the same speech he also dealt with understanding, as Israel Sieff had done in his first speech in the House of Lords in 1966, when he pointed to 'the need for a special attitude of mind on the part of those engaged in industry and commerce', which lay 'at the core of our economic problem'. 'To break down the element of fear, suspicion, and insecurity is a very difficult thing to do when dealing with human relations', he went on, 'but it has to be done if industry is to reach the high degree of efficiency which we all desire'.

Neither Simon Marks nor Marcus Sieff liked talking about 'industrial relations'. The term suggested, they maintained, that there was a conflict between 'two sides' and a necessary confrontation. They chose instead to talk of 'human relations in industry', and preferred to evolve their own policies rather than argue about what either trade unions or the state might proscribe. When he spoke to the Institute of Directors in 1969, with Barbara Castle on one side of him and Ronald Reagan (then Governor of California) on the other, on 'Human Relations – Success or Failure?', Marcus Sieff insisted that he was not just talking about good industrial relations or good communications between management and staff, important though they were. These would largely 'fall into line' if human relations were good. In a later talk of 1980 to the Headmasters' Conference, he was explicit about the difference between the term 'good human relations' and the common term 'industrial relations'. 'We are human beings at work', he went on, 'not industrial beings'. It is a judgement he has repeated on many occasions. Lord Sieff rightly felt that he had inherited this philosophy and did not invent it. According to Simon Marks, Israel Sieff had always been interested in social questions, and 'it was he who made me realise what a terrible part is played in people's lives by fear and insecurity and how much people are affected by them in business'.

As M & S has grown into a big twentieth-century business, with strong managerial initiative, it has always insisted on retaining the philosophy of a smaller family business and it has always tried to ensure that the individual within it is not lost in the machine. 'It's still a family business', Lord Sieff explained in March 1983, a few months before his seventieth birthday, when he announced that he was handing over the role of Chief Executive to Lord Rayner. 'An important part of the business is its family spirit'.

Lord Rayner, Chairman and Chief Executive of M & S.

As this book has shown, that spirit runs through the enterprise and is not associated only with 'the top'. It permeates – and has permeated – the whole organisation. Good feeling expresses itself: it is not induced. 'Here at Winchester Store', Frank Bailey, a warehouseman, wrote in 1967 in an article called 'We're an M & S family', 'my married sister Mrs Flux is the Staff Manageress, another sister, Brenda, is an Invoice Clerk, and yet another sister, Pearl, is a junior Window Dresser. My wife is also in the office, and I'm in the Warehouse, so now we are five'. At the bus stop on their way to the store neighbours would call out, 'There goes the M & S Platoon'. 'I'm often asked', Mr Bailey went on, 'what it's like to work, day in, day out, with so many of one's family. I always reply that each one of us has different duties to perform and that we're all happy in our work. I can assure you that there isn't much that goes on here from the sales floor to the very roof, that we Baileys don't know about'. (The Baileys, it should be added, were one seventh of the total work-force at Winchester.)

When Alec Taylor retired as manager of Hull/Bridlington in February 1983, he wrote to Lord Sieff:

> 'Thank you very much indeed for taking the trouble to talk to me on the telephone today and to wish me good luck in my years of retirement... There is no real substitute for the very top man talking to you... The highlight of the year was when you or your uncle or your father telephoned the store and probed the health of the takings, the health of the staff and the health of the business in general... It is a subject on which I feel very intensely and which I hold to be the real secret of success of our Family Business.'

Each M & S store has its own distinctive character, but each too is expected to follow M & S philosophy. The mobility of managers ensures the circulation of ideas and practices, and staff in one store are encouraged to discover what is going on in other stores. A note in *Sparks* as early as 1939 read: 'If you want to correspond with anyone in any other store all you have to do is to send your name and address (and age) to the Welfare Department'. And this idea was suggested by a sales assistant at Salisbury.

One purpose of placing the emphasis on the individual within M & S has been to give the able, hardworking and creative employee the chance to do well within M & S. At the same time it has been necessary to spotlight 'the ladder of success' in M & S in order to draw in people of intelligence and drive who might otherwise never have wished to join a retailing concern, however enterprising. M & S

Above: Lord Marks, Chairman of M & S from 1916 to 1964.

Below: J. Edward Sieff, who joined M & S at Simon Marks's invitation in 1933 and was Chairman from 1967 to 1972

individualism does not stop at that point, however. Every individual has to know what is going on in the business – very little is deemed to be confidential – and every individual has her or his needs recognised. 'Top management', Lord Sieff has stated simply, 'must have the right mental attitude, which must be based on a sincere respect for the individual'. 'A business, to be worthwhile', the present Lord Sieff has written, 'must have a soul'.

'Leadership' in M & S – and it is considered essential, if principles are to be implemented – must be 'just leadership', a leadership based on shared experience, a sense of responsibility and, increasingly, on proper training, for, as a *St Michael News* headline put it in 1967, 'Training Begins at the Top'. Communication is essential also. As long ago as 1924, on returning from his visit to the United States, Simon Marks felt that it was his first task 'to impart the philosophy of our evolving business to our executives. They must know the why and the wherefore; why we must be selective and discriminating; why production must be responsive to consumer demand'. And in 1980 Marcus Sieff wrote that 'management must always know what working conditions are like on the factory and shop floor'. 'They cannot know how good or bad staff amenities are unless they make use of them themselves ... If the amenities are not good enough for those in charge, they are not good enough for any employee'.

The second task which Simon Marks identified in 1924 was, significantly, to develop 'a close collaboration with our manufacturers, who should be regarded as partners ... whose good will should be obtained and worked for'. It is remarkable how plainly this task was identified by Simon Marks at that time, for M & S had not yet reached the stage where it could be thought of, even in embryo, as a 'manufacturer without factories'.

There was, indeed, an older philosophy of retailing and related manufacturing which was prevalent during the 1920s and which was expressed in a 1930 letter from a Torquay shopkeeper to the *Shoe and Leather Record*: 'The white season trade of shoe retailers is likely to meet with a setback. In this town, a firm are offering tennis shoes, bathers and plimsolls at slaughter prices. Such a state of things should not be allowed to exist. The remedy is in the factors' hands, who, with the cooperation of retailers, should refuse to handle the goods of manufacturers who supply chain stores'.

Such a restrictive philosophy, designed to protect retailer and producer, leaves the customer out of the equation. The M & S philosophy, as we have seen, has always brought the customer in. And over the years, by precept and by example, M & S have spread their philosophy and their practice to their own suppliers, old and new. From the 1930s onwards M & S buying policy was never *just* a buying policy: it was a 'collaboration'. M & S began by interpreting the customers' needs to the supplier and seeking to improve the quality of the product; but, as the years went by, suppliers began to go directly into the M & S stores themselves in order to assess customers' reactions. Norman Sussman, for example, does this regularly in order to judge reactions to shirts. So also – on Saturdays, in particular – does Peter Wolff, Joint Chief Executive of the highly successful clothing manufacturers S.R. Gent. Simon Marks could have done no more.

Likewise, the M & S welfare philosophy, evangelised to the suppliers, became their own philosophy, modified in the light of their own line of business. In the beginning there was a kind of training, as well as mutual discussion on visits.

'Suppliers Learn About Staff Relations' was a characteristic heading in *St Michael News* in 1971, above a report on a seminar on 'human relations in industry' attended by 29 invited M & S manufacturers, representing the textile, footwear and food sections of the business. That was stage one. By 1982, however, the M & S philosophy had become the accepted philosophy not only of businesses like Dewhirst or Corah, but of new businesses.

The idea of comparing sales assistants with surgeons was characteristic of M & S, and the approach was warmly praised in an article on 'Clean Food' in the monthly industrial magazine *Scope* in 1958, the year when M & S introduced a no-smoking rule in its stores. 'M & S are noteworthy', it stated, 'for having set themselves a standard higher than those advocated in the general propaganda campaigns or enforced in the most enlightened municipalities'.

It would be a mistake to describe the M & S philosophy of business as sentimental or as starry-eyed, for as Marcus Sieff, then Vice-Chairman, told the 1971 Conference on Human Relations in Industry, 'For this Company, looking after our staff has always resulted in higher productivity'. Indeed, it was because of the economic efficiency of M & S as a business that people outside it, including people outside business altogether, paid increasing attention to the M & S credo during the 1960s and 1970s, when it was being recited at Westminster as well as at Baker Street. Increasingly M & S was held up as a model, whichever government was in power. And the Press took up the story. 'Many businessmen in Britain', the editor of *Achievement* wrote in 1966, 'regard M & S as the yardstick by which to judge the efficiency of their own company'. Already by that date a Conservative MP, Hugh Fraser, had remarked in the House of Commons that if the M & S 'Operation Simplification' were adopted by the Civil Service, there would be a saving of over 500,000 million forms and 4,000 tons of paper, 'nearly ninepence off the income tax'; and the Organisation and Methods Division of the Treasury had congratulated M & S on 'a most refreshing approach to the problem of excess paper work'.

This was a prelude to the secondment of four government supply officers, 'Men from the Ministries', to M & S in 1967, where they interviewed staff and studied techniques and procedures. They also imbibed M & S philosophies, for as one of them put it, 'In spite of the size of your organisation, it bears the stamp of a family firm: there is a basic philosophy which leads both to cohesion and simplification in Company affairs'. They felt, indeed, that they had gained both in knowledge and in understanding.

Their visit was the prelude to the secondment of M & S staff to the Civil Service, not least Derek (later Lord) Rayner, who in 1979 was appointed adviser to the Prime Minister in the government's drive to improve efficiency and eliminate waste in Whitehall, a position he gave up at the end of 1982.

There was, in fact, an M & S presence at Westminster as well as at Whitehall. Simon Marks, who had been given a knighthood in 1944, became the first M & S peer 17 years later. 'I was delighted to be given a knighthood', he observed. 'I fancied myself as a knight succouring distressed maidens. A peerage rather reminded me of "Bold bad barons".' Yet the House of Lords gave both Lord Marks and two Lords Sieff the chance of talking sense to an audience different from that on their own or their suppliers' payrolls. The first Lord Sieff's first speech in the House of Lords was on productivity. The second Lord Sieff's first

The M & S policy of selling, as far as possible, only British-made goods is long-established: this advertisement appeared in the *Marks & Spencer Magazine* of Summer 1932.

Lord (Israel) Sieff, Chairman of M & S from 1964 to 1967.

speech included the sentence, 'The creation of wealth for all to share demands a high working performance from everyone'.

They knew, of course, that the working performance within their own business was outstanding, so that when they were speaking they had behind them a hidden constituency – which is not always the case in the House of Lords. Yet within M & S efficiency has never been pursued as a single goal in itself. It has always been associated with care and concern. And there has been far greater continuity inside M & S, however great the changes in society, than there has been in government – from Gladstone to Mrs Thatcher. Never was the continuity better demonstrated than when the widow of the joint founder of M & S, Agnes Spencer, then in her 96th year, set up a Charitable Trust in 1957, designed to support the M & S Benevolent Trust, which Mrs Spencer thought was doing 'wonderful work'. Simon Marks and Israel Sieff were among the signatories to the deed, and through her first gift Mrs Spencer was able to raise the market value of the Benevolent Trust to over £3 million.

This history celebrates the centenary of a company with a philosophy. But there is a very different and characteristic M & S way of celebrating it. The sum of £3½ million has been allocated by the Marks and Spencer board to a charitable Centenary Fund. Staff in each store have selected a local project which they consider would be of lasting benefit to the community, and they have started to raise additional sums of money to support the project. To date more than £500,000 has been raised to supplement the grant from Baker Street. In alphabetical order, the first project, at Aberdeen, is designed to provide additional therapy rooms at a centre for handicapped children, and the last, at York, involves a horticultural training scheme for mentally handicapped young people. Most of the projects are charitable; many are concerned with health, others with the environment, such as the schemes for landscaping the Mound in Princes Street, Edinburgh, and for providing the lighting to illuminate Stirling Castle. All are socially useful, and all have been the result of careful thought. At Macclesfield the project is to help with the creation of a silk museum as part of a Heritage Centre appeal; at Leicester the idea is to support an Age Concern centre for the elderly with a workshop, games room and restaurant, and a guidance service.

The tradition of M & S community giving goes back a long way, and there is continuity there as well as in the business and in its welfare policies. In 1935 a cheque was handed over in Hastings to support a £40,000 appeal for the Hastings Hospital after a 20-minute girls' football match between M & S and Woolworth's; the result was a goal-less draw. (The M & S colours, it was noted, were pale green shirts, khaki shorts, green and yellow belts, and green-topped football socks.) In 1969 staff at Ramsgate stayed late working in the store at Christmas so that the old and disabled could shop in comfort, and they contributed to a fund so that each of these special customers would be given a 7s 6d voucher. In the same year staff at Gloucester raised £116 for food parcels for the old.

When Cyril Naylor described the northern store where he first worked during the 1930s, he firmly placed it in its community – in the High Street, near the centre – and that has always been the right cultural orientation. Indeed M & S has been active in the organisation 'Business in the Community', set up to encourage commercial enterprises to help their local communities. Of course, through charity there has been a national dimension too. For several years M & S employees elected a national Miss Sparks after contests in stores and between divisions, and each Miss Sparks after final selection was given the opportunity of designating a charity of her own choice which would receive money from events associated with her term of office. The Miss Sparks of 1980, Susan Irwin, described the 'fantastic start' she had had to her year when she helped to raise £46,000 for the Riding for the Disabled Association. And at the end of Miss Sparks' year there was a ball to which manufacturers as well as M & S staff were invited.

In 1963 the company donated £1.4 million to charitable causes, including the arts, and a further £600,000 in fashion shows and advertising to aid worthwhile community projects. The total sum made available in 1983 for community work, including secondments, was £2.5 million. Just as important as financial help, there has been help with people. Since 1978 more than 40 staff of M & S have been involved in schemes aimed at job-creation and the training of unemployed teenagers, just as M & S staff have been seconded to the Civil Service. And in this connection Naylor's article on going into his first M & S store in 1932 should be set alongside an article by Janice Morley in the London *Standard* in July 1982 titled 'Executives Who Went Out Into The Cold'.

Alan Dent, a former Army officer, from M & S and Tom Jennings, who had worked for IBM (another company with a philosophy), Janice Morley explained, were 'two men in middle life, middle management, and the middle class'. They were seconded by their companies 'to tackle racial inequality and the problems of young offenders with the intention of generating more jobs for these minority groups … A chastened year later, they see this change of roles as a valuable experience which should be shared by more people'. 'I return to M & S on October 1st', Dent told the author of the article. 'I want to go back, but I don't regret one moment … I shall look at life through a fresh pair of eyes'.

The philosophy of M & S has not changed since the 1930s, but there have been many fresh pairs of eyes, eyes that scan the present and the future not only of M & S but of a whole society. Mine have been fresh eyes, too, looking into the present and the past of M & S and of society, knowing that our sense of the past is itself never fixed. We have to rewrite our histories not every 100 years but every generation.

INDEX

Page numbers in *italics* refer to captions to pictures.

Acknowledgements

The Publishers thank the following organisations for
permission to reproduce the pictures in this book:

Daily Express 102 centre; *Daily Star* 100; Mary Evans
Picture Library 14 bottom right; *South Wales Echo*
102 below; Sun Newspapers 101, 102 above; Topham
Picture Library 12 above left; *Weekend Magazine*
103 above.

The following photographs appear by courtesy of the
Marks and Spencer Archive: 11, 15 below, 18 below
right, 19, 20 below left, 21 below left, 24 below left,
24-5, 26 below, 28 top left and right, 29 above, 30, 31,
33 below centre, 36 below left and right, 37 centre
and below, 38 bottom right and above, 40 above left,
40-1, 41 below right, 42 above, 44, 46 below left and
bottom right, 47, 51 above left, 52 above and below right,
54, 55 above, 56 top left, centre left and below left and
right, 57 left and far right, 59 left and centre right, 61
below left, 65 centre right, 66 below left and above
right, 69 top right, 72, 74, 75, 78 centre left and below
left, 79 above, 81 below, 82, 83 far right and below
left, 86 below left and above and below right, 94 below,
96, 97 below left and top right, 98 below, 99 below, 104
above and below right, 107 above and below left, above
right and below right, 108 below, 109, 111 above, 120,
121, 122, 123 below.

Special photography by Graham Miller: ½ title, title,
8-10, 12 top left, 12-13, 14 above and below left, 16-17,
18 left, 19 above, 20 below left, 21 top and below right,
22-3, 24 above, 25, 26 above, 27, 28 below, 29 below,
30 below, 31 top left, 33 right, 34, 35, 36 above, 37 top,
38 bottom left, 39, 40 below left and above centre,
41 above right and below left, 43, 44 above left, 45, 46
bottom left, 48-50, 51 top left, centre and right, 52 left
and top right, 53, 55 below, 56 bottom, 57 far left and
below right, 58, 59 above right, 60, 61 right, 62-4, 65
above right, 66 above left and below right, 67, 68, 69
left, centre right and below right, 70, 71, 73, 76-7, 78
above left, 79 below, 80, 81 top, 83 top right, 84, 85, 86
top, 87, 93, 94 top, 95, 97 top left, 98 top left, 99 top
right, 104 top, bottom left and far right, 105, 106, 107
above far left and top, 108 above, 112-19, 122 below,
123 above, 124, 125.

Special illustrations by Tony McSweeney

Special Edition Label
The woven label for the front cover of the special edition of this book was produced by the Bell Woven Label Company Limited (Readson Group), Colne, Lancashire, to whom the publishers extend their thanks.